CLASSIC
RACING MOTORCYCLES

The publishers would like to thank the following for their
assistance in the preparation of material appearing in this book:

Ferry Brouwer and fellow organisers of the **Assen Centennial Classic TT**
Roy Richards and staff at the **National Motorcycle Museum**, Birmingham
Gianni Perrone
Sandro Colombo
Richard Rosenthal
Reg Page
Tara Frese
James King

The publishers would also like to thank the following owners and
organisations who loaned their machines for photography:

H.G. Anscheidt, Luciano Battisti, Jaap Blaauwboer, Erwin Bongard,
Rudy van Bortel, Albino Brambilla, Renzo Brioschi, Thomas Burkhardt,
Dieter Busch, Lucio Castelli, Romano Colombo, Jim Curry, CZ Factory,
Ton van Deutekom, Derbi Nacional, Cees van Dongen, J. Geddis / J. Lilley,
Heinz Herz, Herman Herz, Honda Motor Co. Ltd, Borje Jansson,
Willem Knoppert, Joop Koudjis, Alfio Michelli, Sammy Miller, M. Missoni,
National Motorcycle Museum, Louis Nijhof, Oldrich Prokop,
Ivan & Graham Rhodes, Martyn Simpkins, John Surtees / Ubaldo Elli,
Team Elli, Zdenek Tichy, Carlo Ubbiali, Chris Wilson,
Yamaha Motor Co.Ltd, Karl Zimmerman

Every effort has been made to include everyone who assisted in preparing
this book, but we apologise for any inadvertent errors or omissions.

CLASSIC
RACING MOTORCYCLES

MICK DUCKWORTH

CONTENTS IN CHRONOLOGICAL ORDER

All text by: Mick Duckworth
Photographer: Richard Dangerfield
Design: John Gilland
Managing Editor: Andrew Kemp
Production: Lauren Roberts

First published in 2002
by Duke
PO Box 46, Isle of Man, British Isles IM99 1DD

ISBN 0 9529325 1 2

British Library CIP Data
A catalogue record for this book is available
from the British Library

Copyright © 2002
Duke and Warrender Grant Publications Ltd

Design and editorial:
Warrender Grant Publications Ltd
13 Charlotte Mews, London W1T 4EJ

Printed and bound by The Iberian Print Group
7A Arundel Terrace, Brighton, Sussex,
BN2 1GA, United Kingdom

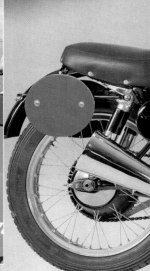

CONTENTS BY MANUFACTURER

FOREWORD

Although it is over 42 years since I retired from competitive motorcycle racing, I have retained an avid fascination for the history and evolution of the racing motorcycle. So it was with eager anticipation that I awaited the proofs of *Classic Racing Motorcycles* – and I was not to be disappointed.

The superb quality of the photographs of many hitherto almost-forgotten machines bristling with inventive features are all supported by a text that serves to remind me of the work of some brilliant designers and engineers, and demonstrates that very little, if anything, is really new. With engine design, in particular, it seems to me that many great ideas were ahead of their time and were perhaps discarded due to the lack of the right materials (not a problem these days). Nevertheless, Rudge machines were highly successful in the 1930s with four-valve cylinder heads, and their 250 helped to propel Graham Walker, a big man, to his one and only TT win.

The gifted designers of the past, such as Giulio Carcano of Moto Guzzi, or Leo Kusmicki and Rex McCandless of Norton, used slide-rules, not computers – plus a lot of flair – to make their calculations. Yet Leo's work for Norton included developing the 'squish' combustion technology (later used in the Vanwall GP car) which, along with his many other contributions, gave the Norton its *third* lease of life, while the brilliant Rex's 'Featherbed' frame used a combination of steering geometry, rigidity, and weight reduction to transform the handling of a bike that to this day is the yardstick used in racing and production frame design.

With stories like these, I am sure that, like me, any motorcycle enthusiast will be enthralled by the visual impact and fascinating text of *Classic Racing Motorcycles*.

Geoff Duke OBE
SIX TIMES WORLD CHAMPION

INTRODUCTION

To succeed in world championship motorcycle road racing takes supreme skill, sheer guts, a touch of luck and perhaps above all, competitive machinery. Even the most talented rider needs the best equipment and team support to gain consistent results and the daunting technical challenge has always been part of Grand Prix racing's fascination.

Since the Fédération Internationale Motocycliste (FIM) initiated the world championships in 1949, dozens of large and small manufacturers have sought glory in the annual season of GP races. Through doing so they have promoted their brands and reaped technical benefits that ultimately made commercial products more sophisticated and reliable.

Over more than 50 years an amazing array of designs has come to the start line in the various classes. Some have been more successful than others, but all possess the purity of purpose and raw functionality that give a Grand Prix machine its special appeal.

In the pages that follow, 60 historic solo GP contenders of 33 makes are described. Presented in chronological order, they chart decades of progress in engine and chassis technology spurred on by relentless competition.

A few significant machines dating from before the FIM series started are included for their technical interest. For similar reasons, the last machine in our selection is the unorthodox rotary-engined 1991 Norton briefly admitted as a guest in the 500cc GP class.

In the first ten years of the championships, once-great British racing marques fell behind as competing Italian factories developed high-revving double overhead camshaft four-stroke engines in various forms. But most of them were eventually forced to cut their costly GP budgets, making the 1960s the decade of the ascendant Japanese marques. A fresh round of inter-factory rivalry fuelled rampant innovation, resulting in the development of some outstanding four-stroke and two-stroke designs. It was a vibrant period in GP racing, but there was increasing concern that the machines were becoming too remote from affordable showroom motorcycles.

A 1970s shake-up, when the FIM imposed design restrictions, saw exotic designs recede and the production racing machine take prominence. But engine and chassis technology moved on nevertheless and the new formulae allowed smaller teams to taste glory, especially in the lesser capacity classes.

By the 1980s, the four-stroke engine had disappeared and intense development continued as teams searched for the optimum blend of speed and handling, aided by new materials and electronics. Ironically, due to the difficulty of making them environmentally acceptable, two-stroke engines were featuring less and less in makers' showroom models, giving rise to more unease about the commercial relevance of racing programmes.

Although the modern Moto GP series has produced truly epic racing in recent years, the rich technical variety seen in earlier times has been absent. But 2002 sees the launch of the new GP formula admitting four-strokes of up to 990cc, much more like modern showroom machines than the established 500cc two-strokes they will race against. As a result, GP grids should see a welcome return to design diversity.

▶ Gilera's high-revving across-the-frame four reigned supreme in the early 1950s, as Italian factories shattered the early British supremacy.

▼ Bikes such as the NSU pioneered new frame technology, high-tech materials, aerodynamics and advanced engine designs in the quest for speed and good handling.

◀ Norton's tireless development programme kept its simple 500cc Manx single as a prominent contender through into the 1960s.

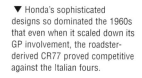

▼ Honda's sophisticated designs so dominated the 1960s that even when it scaled down its GP involvement, the roadster-derived CR77 proved competitive against the Italian fours.

GP history landmarks

1924 -1939
European Championships
mainly for 250cc, 350cc and 500cc classes

1949
FIM world championships inaugurated
for 500cc, 350cc, 250cc, 125cc and sidecar classes

1957
New streamlining rules for solos: both wheels must
be fully visible.

1962
50cc class introduced

1969
New machine formula
50cc: maximum one cylinder, six speeds
125cc: maximum two cylinders, six speeds

1970
New formula extends to bigger classes
250cc: maximum two cylinders, six speeds
350cc: maximum two cylinders, six speeds
500cc: maximum four cylinders, six speeds

1979
For one year, two sidecar championships were run
in parallel: B2A for conventional outfits and B2B
for three-wheeled racing cars.

1983
350cc class dropped

1984
80cc class replaces 50cc

1988
125cc machines limited to one cylinder

1990
80cc class dropped

1997
Sidecar class dropped

2002
Four-strokes of up to 990cc join 500cc two-strokes
in premier GP class

AJS V4 1939

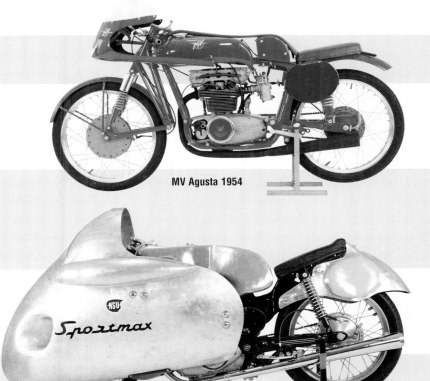

MV Agusta 1954

NSU Sporttmax 251rS 1955

Kawasaki KR500 1981

MOTO GUZZI C4V

499cc · 1926

A sensational victory in the first ever European Championship event at Monza in 1924 established Moto Guzzi as a leading racing marque. The first prototype machine designed by Carlo Guzzi and financed by Giorgio Parodi had only appeared four years earlier, but the fledgling Italian factory lost no time in embarking on a sporting career with its distinctive flat singles. They were to win countless races and break many records in the ensuing years and form the basis for Guzzis that kept the marque at the forefront in GP racing through the 1950s.

The 500cc Guzzi which won the prestigious Monza race in the hands of Guido Mentasta set a pattern for many subsequent models, with its horizontal, radially-finned cylinder, outside flywheel and a gearbox built in unit with the crankcase. Replacing a two valve racer, the 1924 500 followed the original Guzzi prototype in having four valves in its combustion chamber, operated in pairs via rockers from a single shaft-driven overhead camshaft.

Despite having twice as many valves as a typical racing single of the period, the Guzzi was essentially of simple and sturdy design. A two-valve 250 derived from it was Guzzi's first Isle of Man TT entry in 1926 and made an even bigger impression in international racing.

A production version of the 500cc Corsa 4 Valvole (C4V) was made available to selected riders and updated as the 4VTT and then the 4VSS before being discontinued after 1932. The 1926 C4V is essentially similar to the Monza victor, having the engine mounted low in an open-bottomed tubular rigid frame with downtubes passing on either side of the forward-facing cylinder. The girder front fork has a single central coil spring, with damping by an adjustable friction device set ahead of it. The antiquated rim-type front brake was about to be replaced by a drum, as fitted on the rear wheel.

A long curved tract connects the carburettor to the intake port and a single plain exhaust pipe runs along the right side of the machine. The four gear ratios are selected by a hand lever mounted on the right of the wedge-shaped fuel tank: foot-change was still a novelty in 1926.

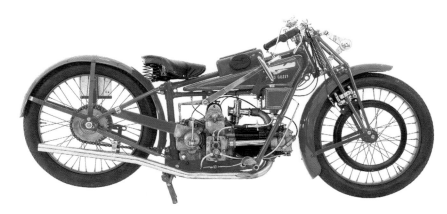

▲ Guzzi's flat single engine layout keeps weight low in the chassis. An external flywheel maintains torque and ignition is by a magneto on top of the crankcase behind the carburettor.

▼ The front brake operates by pressing friction blocks against a spoke-mounted rim. This arrangement was soon replaced by a superior drum brake with internal expanding shoes.

Engine type: Single-cylinder, single-overhead-camshaft, four-valve four-stroke
Capacity: 499cc
Bore and stroke: 88mm x 82mm
Compression ratio: 6:1
Fuel system: 28.5mm Amac carburettor
Power: 22PS @ 5,500rpm
Gearbox: Four-speed
Suspension: Front, girder fork. Rear, none
Brakes: Block and rim front. Rear, drum
Dry weight: 130kg
Top speed: 95mph

ITALIAN INNOVATOR
Guzzi's international victory at Monza in 1924 was a wake-up call to the British factories dominating the 500cc class at the time. Flat singles were raced by the factory until it withdrew from the GPs in 1957.

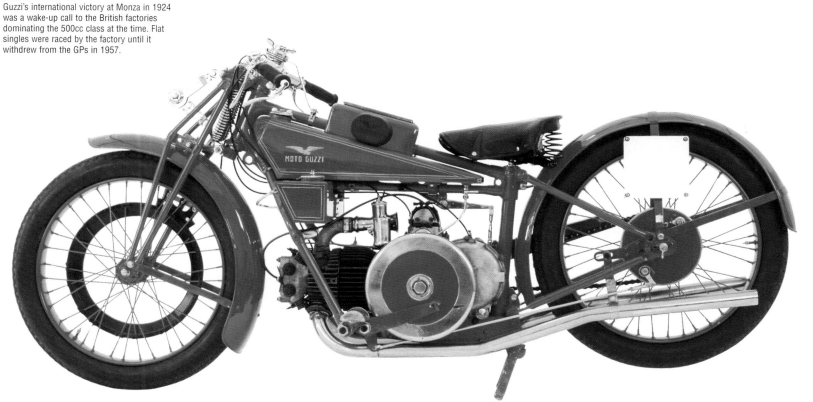

NEW IMPERIAL
246cc · 1935

New Imperial's small-scale works team built up its reputation in the Twenties, scoring 250cc Lightweight TT wins in 1921, 1924 and 1925, plus a 350cc Junior in 1924. The successes kept coming in the following decade, with 250cc victories at the TT and Continental grand prix events in France, Germany and Holland during 1932. And in the same year a New Imperial single made the first quarter-litre 100mph lap of the Brooklands circuit in Surrey in the hands of Les Archer.

The Birmingham factory's 1936 250cc Lightweight TT win was the last in that event by an all-British machine. Works rider Bob Foster notched a surprise first place after TT legend Stanley Woods' supercharged DKW two-stroke retired when leading.

The 1936 season was also the final stand in that class for engines with overhead valves operated by pushrods and chassis with unsuspended rigid rear ends. But, unusually for a British machine, Foster's engine had a gearbox built in unit with the engine, with primary drive by gears.

The 250cc TT and European Championship series in the remaining years before WWII would be the preserve of Italian overhead camshaft four-strokes and German two-strokes with supercharging, all with fully-sprung frames.

Other New Imperial works racers of the period, including Ginger Wood's 1936 250cc Ulster GP-winning mount had separate gearboxes with chain primary drive, as seen on this 1935 example. Its engine is of dated design with a vertical air-cooled cylinder and camshafts on the right side of the crankcase, operating two valves via pushrods and rockers on top of the cylinder head. Readily changeable hairpin valve springs replaced the simple coil type used previously.

Mixture is fed from the carburettor to the inlet valve by an intake tract angled for optimum gas flow. Ignition is by a magneto mounted behind the cylinder and because engine tuning was narrowing the useful power band, New Imperial was among the first makes to fit mechanical rev counters. Oil for the dry sump lubrication system is stored in a frame-mounted tank, with a long filler neck to accept a funnel during pit stops.

▲ The tubular steel frame is of duplex loop construction and, despite the lack of rear suspension, the New Imperial had fine handling by the standards of the time.

▼ Use of cool-running, light aluminium-alloy castings instead of iron for the cylinder and head was an advanced feature. The cylinder has an iron liner and the head uses a bronze insert.

Engine type: Single-cylinder, air-cooled, pushrod two-valve four-stroke
Capacity: 246cc
Bore and stroke: 62.5 x 80mm
Compression ratio: 10.5:1
Fuel system: Amal TT carburettor
Power: not available
Gearbox: Four-speed
Suspension: Front: girder front fork. Rear, none
Brakes: Drums front and rear
Dry weight: not available
Top speed: 95mph

LAST OF THE OLD-SCHOOL LIGHTWEIGHTS
The New Imperial works racers built in 1935 were the last before the factory's demise. The marque had won four 250cc TTs and one 350cc event, as well as numerous European races.

RUDGE FOUR-VALVE

499cc · 1935

Rudge Whitworth's racing involvement began before World War I, but the marque really came to the fore at the end of the Twenties as the first British factory to score international road racing successes using a four-valve combustion chamber. Designed by factory development engineer George Hack, innovative Rudge singles won three Isle of Man TTs, two Ulster GPs and were prominent on the European grand prix circuit until the mid-1930s.

Using paired, rather than single, inlet and exhaust valves enhanced engine breathing and made it possible to locate the spark plug centrally for better combustion. Additional benefits were lighter reciprocating parts in the valve train and exhaust valves that dissipated heat more rapidly.

Rudge rider Graham Walker was leading the 1928 Senior TT when his engine failed, but he made amends by winning the next two Ulster GPs in 1928-9, averaging over 80mph in both races on the formidable Clady circuit.

A TT Senior and Junior double victory was achieved in 1930. A 350cc version had joined the 500 and the previously untried smaller engine took a sensational 1-2-3 victory in the Junior event. It had four valves set radially around the plug in a hemispherical chamber, rather than parallel pairs in a 'pent-roof' head.

Applied to a 250cc engine, the ingenious pushrod-operated radial system gained Rudge another first three placing in the 1934 Lightweight TT, headed by Walker, who ran a 'works' team despite the factory's official withdrawal from racing in the previous year.

On its post-1930 500s, Rudge settled for a simplified radial exhaust and parallel inlet valve layout. The resulting 'semi-radial' engine produced ample power but handled badly as a result. Its best placings were two TT fourths before the company's financial troubles forced it to retire from official racing.

As well as pioneering the four-valve technology that would speed Honda to GP success in the Sixties, Rudge introduced a four-speed gearbox when most of its rivals had only three ratios. The company also pioneered large diameter drum brakes with linked and compensated operation, applying the front drum harder than the rear to avoid locking the wheel.

▲ Parallel inlet valves are opened by rockers on a transverse shaft, actuated by the rearmost pushrod. The other pushrod operates the radial exhaust valves via a train of rockers.

▼ Unusually large for a British racer of the time, the 203mm brake drums contain shoes with a generous area of friction material. They are expanded by a cam to contact the iron liner.

Engine type: Single-cylinder, air-cooled, pushrod four-valve four-stroke
Capacity: 499cc
Bore and stroke: 85 x 88mm
Compression ratio: 7.5 :1
Fuel system: Amac carburettor
Power: 28PS @ 6,000rpm
Gearbox: Four-speed
Suspension: Front: girder front fork. Rear: none
Brakes: Drums front and rear
Dry weight: n/a
Top speed: 110mph

PRESCRIPTION FOR BETTER BREATHING
Rudge raised the engine game with its four-valve singles. But by 1935, the date of this machine, overhead camshaft four-strokes had become dominant in international racing.

AJS V4

495cc · 1939

B y far the most technically adventurous of Britain's pre-war grand prix racers, the 500cc V4 fielded by AJS in 1939 used supercharging for maximum power and liquid-cooling to ensure reliability.

Based on an earlier air-cooled four adapted from a roadster design, the complex but potent 80PS AJS power unit has its pairs of cylinders set in a 50-degree vee. The five-bearing crankshaft's two big-end journals are spaced at 180 degrees, each carrying one plain and one forked connecting rod. A chain takes primary drive to the separate Burman four speed gearbox and the compressor, also chain driven, mounts ahead of the crankcase.

Reduction gears at the crankshaft centre turn the camshaft drive sprocket at half engine speed. A long chain takes drive to single camshafts on each head, where rockers operate the two valves in each cylinder.

Ignition is by a pair of magnetos, held in clamps and bevel-driven off the right side of the crankshaft, while fuel mixture is supplied by a single Amal carburettor mounted on the top of the Zoller supercharger. Oil for the dry sump system is carried in a tank on the right side of the frame. Liquid-cooling makes it possible to arrange all four exhaust ports and their plain pipes at the rear of the cylinders.

Surprisingly compact and measuring less than 410mm (16in) across, the power unit sits in a double cradle tubular frame. Suspension is conventional for the period, with a girder front fork and plunger springing at the rear.

While the AJS proved very fast in a straight line, its handling could be hair-raising. Even so, brave works pilot Walter Rusk wrestled his unruly four round the Ulster GP's bumpy Clady Course at an astonishing lap average of 100mph. After holding an early lead, the Irish rider was forced to retire when a fork link sheared under the strain.

The 1939 Ulster GP showing demonstrated that the 135mph AJS could be competitive against Gilera's liquid-cooled, supercharged in-line four, which won that race and the last European Championship run before World War Two. When GP racing resumed and the FIM World championship series was inaugurated for 1949, supercharging was banned.

▲ The 21in front wheel is equipped with an effective 190mm twin-leading-shoe drum brake. The cooling system's impeller pump can be seen on the side of the crankcase.

▼ Water cooling was adopted after the air-cooled version suffered cylinder distortion. The twin oil pumps are inside the triangular casing between the two magnetos.

Engine type: V-four, liquid-cooled, dohc, two-valve four-stroke
Capacity: 495cc
Bore and stroke: 50mm x 63mm
Compression ratio: 7.9:1
Fuel system: Single Amal carburettor, supercharger
Power: 80PS
Gearbox: Four-speed
Suspension: Front, girder fork. Rear, plungers
Brakes: Drums front and rear
Dry weight: 190kg
Top speed: 135mph

TOO HOT TO HANDLE
With tremendous power that outstripped its roadholding capability, the four-cylinder 500cc AJS was the only supercharged British factory racer to reach a grand prix starting grid. Its career was cut short by World War Two.

BMW TYPE 255

492cc · 1939

First wheeled out in 1935, BMW's supercharged double overhead camshaft flat twin went on to be a 500cc class leader, proved when the lightweight shaft-driven German machines stormed to convincing first and second places at record speed in the 1939 Isle of Man Senior TT, ridden by Georg Meier and Jock West.

Although it shares the air-cooled, horizontally opposed twin cylinder format traditionally seen on BMW roadsters, the Type 255's engine is a pure racing unit with magnesium alloy castings and camshaft drive by shafts and bevel gears. The vane-type Zoller supercharger is built into the front of the crankcase and turned at engine speed by the nose of the longitudinal crankshaft. Inhaling mixture through a Fischer-Amal carburettor, the compressor delivers it to the inlet tracts via tubes curving under the cylinders.

A magneto on top of the crankcase provides ignition sparks and a reservoir below it contains oil for the wet-sump lubrication system. With the two cylinders and sump well exposed, efficient air cooling is achieved.

The flat twin layout also keeps weight distribution usefully low in the lightweight all-welded tubular frame. BMW pioneered telescopic fork front suspension with coil springs and hydraulic damping, which provided relative rider comfort, important in long races over road courses. Spring plungers are fitted at the rear with friction dampers thought to be a later addition. A linked braking system is used, with the 200mm drum front brake operated by cables from both the handlebar lever and the right-side foot pedal that also brings on the rear drum.

Shaft drive makes changes to overall gearing more awkward than simply changing chain drive sprockets, but the BMW team fitted alternative bevel gears to suit different circuits.

In July 1939, Meier set the first-ever 100mph lap of a road circuit at Spa Francorchamps, Belgium. But BMW's hopes of achieving total invincibility in the premier 500cc class were dashed when Gilera arrived on the scene with its devastating 85bhp liquid-cooled blown four. The Italian factory wrested the 1939 500cc European championship from BMW.

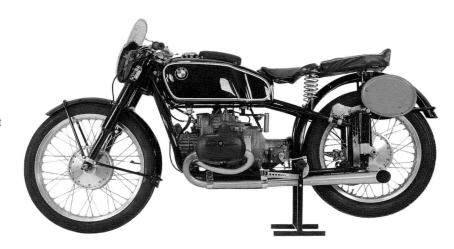

▲ Weight is kept low in the chassis, with the blower at the front of the crankcase. An emergency plug spanner is carried above the four speed gearbox housing.

▼ Unusually for a racing machine, final drive is by shaft with universal joints and bevel gears. Chain drives of the 1930s often flung oil onto the rear tyre in a long race.

Engine type: Flat twin, air-cooled, double-overhead-camshaft, two-valve four-stroke
Capacity: 492cc
Bore and stroke: 66mm x 72mm
Compression ratio: 5:1
Fuel system: 27mm Fischer-Amal carburettor, Zoller supercharger
Power: 55PS @ 7000rpm
Gearbox: Four-speed
Suspension: Front, telescopic fork. Rear, plungers
Brakes: Drums front and rear
Dry weight: 137kg
Top speed: 130mph

TOTAL PACKAGE
The BMW Type 255 flat twin achieved European championship success through its blend of power and manageability. Even with supercharging, dry weight is only 137kg.

DKW
349cc · 1939

Reputed to be the noisiest machines in the history of road racing, DKW two-strokes were at the cutting edge of technology in the 1930s. The German single and twin-cylinder racers featured liquid-cooling, twin-bore cylinders with common combustion chambers and additional supercharging pistons to deliver incoming mixture under higher pressure than was possible with a normally aspirated engine.

DKW's huge racing department employed 200 people and works riders won several 250 and 350cc European championships as well as the 1938 250cc TT, while batches of production racers were made available for privateers. The last produced before World War II was the SS350 of 1939, of which no more than 25 examples were made. A double-piston 'split twin', the four-speed SS350 was closer to works specification than DKW's other production racers and with 36PS, it was the most powerful 350 that could be bought.

The engine has two combustion chambers topping twin-bore cylinders with four pistons side-by-side in pairs on a common crankshaft. Using double bores, with transfer ports from the crankcase controlled by one piston and the exhaust port by the other, allowed asymmetrical timing not possible with a normal piston-port two-stroke. Induction to the crankcase via piston-controlled ports in the rear bores is by 22mm carburettors and supercharging by a single large-diameter 'Ladepumpe' piston sited under the crankshaft and linked to it by a third connecting rod. A flywheel generator powers the ignition.

Conventional for its time, the double cradle frame features plunger rear suspension and carries a friction-damped girder fork at the front. The drum brakes are in full-width wheel hubs. The large aluminium fuel tank, dictated by the two-stroke's prodigious thirst, has outlets at its lowest point towards the rear. Oil was pre-mixed with the fuel. Gearchange is a by a foot pedal on the right and the tiny sprung saddle has a mudguard-mounted pad behind it, used by riders when crouching low to cut wind resistance along straights. Well placed to catch cooling air, the radiator is mounted between the frame's front downtubes.

▲ Distinctive in appearance, noisy and thirsty for fuel, DKW's liquid-cooled SS350 split-twin two-stroke was closely related to the UL350 works team machine.

▼ Twin carburettors are tucked between the splayed rear-facing exhaust pipes, with induction timing controlled by piston-ports in the rear cylinders' bores.

Engine type: Twin-cylinder, liquid-cooled, piston-port two-stroke
Capacity: 349cc
Bore and stroke: 39.5mm x 68.5mm
Compression ratio: n/a
Fuel system: Two carburettors, supercharger
Power: 36PS @ 7,000rpm
Gearbox: Four-speed
Suspension: Front, girder fork. Rear, plungers
Brakes: Drums front and rear
Dry weight: 145kg
Top speed: 110mph

POWER THROUGH COMPLEXITY
Of complex design with a total of five pistons, including the compressor pump under the crankcase, the 36PS DKW was the most powerful 350 available to privateers in 1939, but few were able to buy it.

NSU KOMPRESSOR

347cc · 1939

Although less successful than BMW and DKW, NSU played an important role in Germany's drive to dominate international racing in the 1930s. The flourishing factory in Neckarsulm, Germany, had been involved in racing since 1905 and took on former Norton designer Walter Moore in 1929. His ohc NSU singles were competitive, but were superseded by the more ambitious supercharged 350cc parallel twin.

Weighty and tall, with slightly inclined air-cooled cylinders, the NSU's engine has a 180-degree crankshaft and individual shaft and bevel drives for each of its twin overhead camshafts. Two valves in each combustion chamber are closed by hairpin-type springs. A single carburettor supplies mixture to the supercharger, located over a gearbox built in unit with the engine and driven by gears. Primary drive is by chain in an enclosed oil bath on the left side, with another chain drive for the wet sump lubrication system's pump. The final drive chain is on the right. An ignition magneto is sited ahead of the heavily finned crankcase.

The tubular frame has widely spaced downtubes, allowing engine weight to be set well forward. Suspension is by a girder front fork and rear plungers, although some team riders preferred a rigid rear end. Huge 36-litre fuel tanks of hand-beaten aluminium were fitted to deal with the engine's prodigious thirst for fuel and their rear portions were formed to keep weight low.

The twin debuted at the Sachsenring in 1938, where works rider Heiner Fleischmann found it lacked cornering clearance, a problem which was addressed by fitting high-level exhausts. A team of revised 350s contested the 1939 Isle of Man TT, where Fleischmann took third place in the Junior race. But despite an output of 68PS which put them ahead on sheer power, the NSUs were overweight and unreliable. The outbreak of World War II halted the further development they needed.

There were also 250 and 500cc versions, the latter making 98PS. The twins reappeared after the war to compete in German national events where supercharging was permitted. A supercharged 500cc NSU streamliner raised the absolute motorcycle speed record to over 210mph in 1956.

▲ The primary chain, clutch and supercharger drive are enclosed. Upswept exhausts were fitted to overcome a lack cornering clearance, with heat shields to protect riders's legs.

▼ Driven by gears off the transmission, the vane-type compressor draws mixture through a single carburettor and delivers it under pressure to conventionally-placed inlet tracts.

Engine type: Parallel twin, air-cooled, double-overhead-camshaft, two-valve four-stroke
Capacity: 347cc
Bore and stroke: 56mm x 70.5mm
Compression ratio: n/a
Fuel system: Carburettor and supercharger
Power: 68PS @ 8,500rpm
Gearbox: Four-speed
Suspension: Front, girder fork. Rear, plunger
Brakes: Drums front and rear
Dry weight: 200kg
Top speed: 125mph

WEIGHT PENALTY
NSU's supercharged 347cc dohc twin cylinder engine gave plenty of power, but the machine was overweight at 200kg and World War II interrupted development. More refined unblown NSU twins would gain GP success in the 1950s.

VELOCETTE ROARER

498cc · 1939

Velocette's chief designer Harold Willis coined the Roarer nickname for the supercharged twin that the British company designed to take on the best grand prix 500s of the late 1930s. Designed between 1938 and 1939, the Velocette had some similarities with the then-dominant BMW, being a shaft-drive twin, but its engine layout was wholly innovative.

Willis felt that BMW's horizontally opposed engine was too wide, and though it offered smooth running, the gyroscopic effect of its longitudinal crankshaft affected handling. His solution was a vertical twin using two contra-rotating cranks geared to each other with their pistons rising and falling together. As a result, all the forces cancel each other out, resulting in perfect balance with no adverse gyroscopic effect. The left crankshaft drives the clutch and gearbox, while the right shaft turns a Centric six-blade compressor and the ignition magneto.

Separate cylinder heads with single bevel-driven overhead camshafts are arranged with rearward facing exhausts, a layout adopted when liquid cooling was envisaged. But air cooling was chosen for the final design, so aluminium ducts are used to route cool air to the exhaust ports. Despite the Roarer name, the sound from its straight-through pipes is surprisingly subdued.

A long induction tract conducts mixture from the supercharger to the forward facing inlet ports, running over the cam boxes. Engine oil is stored in a well-cooled streamlined casing ahead of the crankcase.

Despite extensive use of lightweight magnesium alloy, the Roarer still weighs a hefty 168kg, thanks to twin crankshafts and the supercharger.

For testing under racing conditions, the Roarer was ridden during 1939 TT practice by Velocette's brilliant works rider Stanley Woods. He was impressed by a broad power band, smooth running and exceptionally stable handling, while Velocette had high hopes of raising power output for European Championship success in 1940. Unfortunately, World War Two intervened and the Roarer was never raced. With supercharging banned in postwar grand prix racing, Velocette reverted to conventional singles before withdrawing its race team altogether after 1952.

▲ Aluminium ducting is used to direct cool air to the rearward-facing exhaust ports and the engine oil reservoir in the crankcase nose is well positioned for cooling

▼ Shaft drive is BMW-inspired and suits the engine layout, but swingarm rear suspension was pioneered in grand prix racing by the Velocette factory.

Engine type: Vertical twin, twin-crank, ohc four-stroke
Capacity: 498cc
Bore and stroke: 68mm x 68.25mm
Compression ratio: 7.5:1
Fuel system: Carburettor and supercharger
Power: 62PS
Gearbox: Four-speed
Suspension: Front: girder fork. Rear, swingarm with twin shocks
Brakes: Drums front and rear
Dry weight: 168kg
Top speed: 140mph

BALANCING ACT
Velocette chose the unorthodox, well-balanced contra-rotating parallel twin cylinder layout to achieve superior handling as well as power. More development might have brought the Roarer international success.

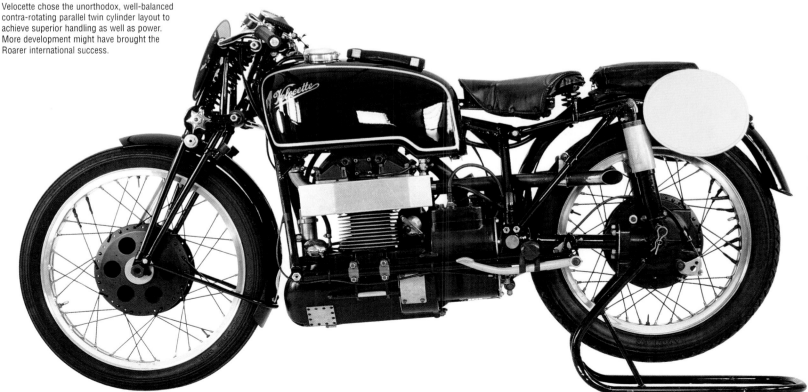

VELOCETTE KTT MKVIII

348CC · 1947

Britain's Velocette factory dominated the 350cc class in the years preceding and following World War II. The small family firm's K-series overhead camshaft singles evolved from a 350 which gained Velocette's first big win at the 1926 Junior TT. In the late thirties, Velocettes became the mainstay of 350cc grids in international events and works machines won five out of five Junior TTs between 1938 and 1949. A number of 350cc KTT racing models had been made available to privateers since the 1920s, with major updates from MkI to the MkVIII of 1939. Their popularity and competitiveness can be gauged by the fact that in 1939, 25 out of the first 35 places in the 1939 Junior TT were taken by Velocette mounted riders. Supplies of a revived 350cc KTT MkVIII resumed in 1947, when it was one of the few genuine racing machines available to privateers. But after winning the 1949 and 1950 350cc world championships, Velocette opted out of costly GP involvement.

The MkVIII's engine is closely based on the works type, with a narrow, rigid crankcase and extensive finning on the cylinder and head for efficient cooling. Drive to the single camshaft is by a shaft and bevel gears on the right side of the cylinder. The two valves are opened by rockers and closed by hairpin valve springs. In the 1930s, compression ratios of up to 11: 1 were used, but in the immediate postwar period UK racers were forced to used low-octane petrol, requiring a lower ratio of 7.5: 1. Carburation is by a down-draughted Amal TT instrument and ignition sparks generated by a chain-driven BTH magneto mounted behind the cylinder. Oil for the dry sump lubrication system is stored in a tank fixed to the frame below the seat and circulated by a crankshaft-driven pump with pipes and jets arranged to deliver oil to the upper bevel gears and cams.

Unusual in combining girder fork front suspension with a swinging arm and twin air-filled shocks at the rear, the KTT MkVIII has a tubular frame with a single downtube, branching into twin rails where it runs under the engine and four-speed gearbox. The lower crankcase sits between the bottom rails, helping to keep crankshaft weight low and contributing to the Velocette's admired handling.

▲ A soft pad on the rear mudguard behind the sprung saddle allows the rider to shift weight backwards when crouching low along straights to reduce wind resistance.

▼ Velocette's advanced rear suspension. A swinging arm made in tapered steel tube is controlled by two Dowty air-sprung, oil-damped shock absorber units.

Engine type: Single-cylinder, air cooled, single-overhead-camshaft, two-valve four-stroke
Capacity: 348cc
Bore and stroke: 74mm x 81mm
Compression ratio: 7.5:1
Fuel system: Amal TT carburettor
Power: 32PS @ 7,000rpm
Gearbox: Four-speed
Suspension: Front, girder fork. Rear, swingarm with twin shocks
Brakes: Drums front and rear
Dry weight: 150kg
Top speed: 110mph

FORTIES' FLYER
Despite being virtually a re-isuue of a pre-war machine. the ohc Velocette KTT proved highly competitive for a few seasons. But after 1950, it rapidly faded through lack of development.

AJS 7R
348cc · 1948

▲ The early 7R's fuel tank is secured by four bolts inserted at the sides and covered by bungs. Twin taps supply fuel to the Amal 10TT carburettor's remote float chamber.

Built primarily for privateer racers, the 350cc AJS 7R was intended to be a reliable, easily-maintained tool for private entrants rather than a grand prix front runner. But instant results from the 32PS single launched in 1948 as the 'Boy's Racer' shook rivals and set the 7R on a long and successful track career Taking fourth in that year's Senior 500cc TT, it won numerous Junior Manx Grands Prix and powered GP privateers into the mid-1960s.

Produced at Associated Motor Cycles, owner of the Matchless and AJS brands, the 7R was designed by Philip Walker, guided by AMC sales chief and former BMW works rider Jock West.

For strength, the engine features deeply spigoted head-to-barrel and barrel-to-crankcase joints. And for simplicity a chain-driven single overhead camshaft is used, following a pattern set by pre-war AJS racing singles. The camshaft chain and its Weller tensioner are housed, along with magneto drive gears and twin oil pumps, in a timing case which gives the 7R engine its distinct appearance. Along with the crankcase and cambox castings, the casing is made in lightweight magnesium alloy, and a gold paint is used to prevent oxidisation. A slot in the upper portion of the timing case allows cooling air to exit after flowing crossways over the head.

The rigid tubular double cradle frame has widely spaced downtubes through which the exhaust pipe passes, before terminating in a large megaphone. The front fork is the oil-damped Teledraulic type developed by AMC during World War II and the rear shock absorbers are also of in-house origin. Lightweight conical wheel hubs contain drum brakes, with twin-leading-shoe operation at the front. Thanks to careful design and choice of materials, dry weight is only 132kg.

A 7R-based works three-valve AJS was taken to a Junior TT win by Rod Coleman in 1954 and the production model benefited from ongoing development by Jack Williams at AMC, gaining a sleeker shape, a shorter cylinder stroke and an added 10PS before production ended in 1962. From 1958 it had been joined by the Matchless G50, almost identical to the two-valve 7R except for its 500cc cylinder capacity.

▼ The 1948 version has a huge exhaust megaphone to maximise power at high rpm. Later models used a smaller 'reverse cone' type to gain more flexibility throughout the range.

Engine type: Single-cylinder, single-overhead-camshaft, two-valve four-stroke
Capacity: 348cc
Bore and stroke: 74mm x 81mm
Compression ratio: 8.45:1
Fuel system: 29mm Amal 10TT carburettor
Power: 32PS @ 6500rpm
Gearbox: Four-speed
Suspension: Front, telescopic fork. Rear, swingarm with twin shocks
Brakes: Drums front and rear
Dry weight: 132kg
Top speed: 120mph

SIMPLE SINGLE
Simplicity, lightness and durability are the AJS 7R's main themes. A series of updates during production resulted in the later version being outwardly almost identical to the Matchless G50 (see page 41).

MONDIAL

124cc · 1951

The FB Mondial marque founded by the Boselli brothers dominated the 125cc GP class from 1949 to 1951. The Bologna factory's lightweight four-stroke singles took a hat-trick of convincing world titles, winning every one of eleven 125cc GP rounds and taking 16 podium places during that period. Its champions were all Italian riders: Nello Pagani, Bruno Ruffo and Carlo Ubbiali.

The brilliant engineer behind these successes was Alfonso Drusiani, taken on by Mondial in 1948. He was determined to prove that a high-revving four stroke could be built to defeat the Morini and MV Agusta two-strokes considered unbeatable in postwar Italian national 125 races. Usually raced unstreamlined, the droning blue and silver singles proved too fast for their rivals and both Morini and MV switched to four-stroke power for 1950. Mondial stayed supreme until first MV, and then NSU took over as top 125s.

Drusiani's neat unit-construction 124cc power unit has a vertical shaft with bevel gears on the right side to take drive from the crankshaft to double overhead camshafts via a train of gears in a casing on the right of the cylinder head. On the left of the engine an outside flywheel is concealed in the cover for the geared primary drive and clutch. A remote tank carries oil for the dry sump lubrication system and the gear-driven ignition magneto is located ahead of the crankcase.

Built from light small-diameter tubing, the strong true-handling chassis features rather dated plunger rear suspension and a girder front fork. Both wheels have large diameter 21-inch aluminium rims shod with narrow tyres to cut rolling resistance against the engine's modest 15PS output. Drum brakes of 180mm diameter are fitted front and rear. The seat is a single sprung saddle, with a pad on the streamlined mudguard behind it. FB Mondial's superiority was proved in the first 125cc TT of 1951, when they filled the first three places led by Isle of Man Course specialist Cromie McCandless, signed by the factory for the event.

Development continued and in 1957 Mondial won both the 125 and 250cc world titles with streamlined machines before withdrawing from GP racing.

▲ Light and slim, the machine is built around a tubular double cradle frame with plunger rear suspension. Extensive fairings were fitted for races on faster circuits.

▼ The girder front fork's main members are pressings, acting against a single central coil spring. The efficient front brake has an 180mm diameter drum in a full-width hub.

Engine type: Single-cylinder, air cooled, double-overhead-camshaft, two-valve four-stroke
Capacity: 124cc
Bore and stroke: 53mm x 56mm
Compression ratio: 9.7:1
Fuel system: Dell' Orto carburettor
Power: 15PS @ 11,500rpm
Gearbox: Four-speed
Suspension: Front, girder fork. Rear, plungers
Brakes: Drums front and rear
Dry weight: 85kg
Top speed: 96mph

TWO-STROKE BEATER
Powered by a compact double overhead camshaft engine with a four-speed gearbox, Mondial's 125 single outran its two-stroke contemporaries in grands prix. A much revised version took the 1957 125cc world title.

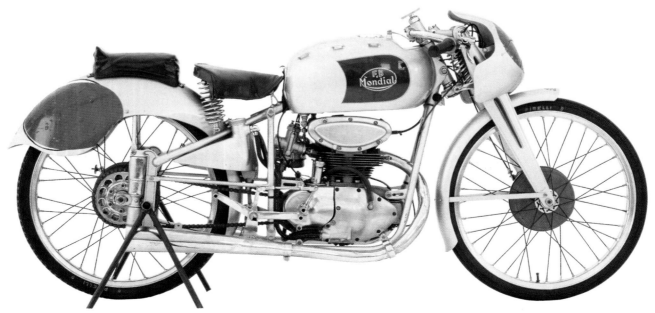

VINCENT GREY FLASH

499cc · 1951

Vincent's Grey Flash evolved from the company's 500cc Comet roadster and was made in tiny numbers for 1950 and 1951. A much livelier machine than the 28PS Comet, the Flash had features in common with Vincent's 1,000cc V-twin Black Lightning racer.

Three works 500s were fielded in the 1950 Senior TT, an enterprise actively encouraged by the Receiver called in to save the ailing Stevenage company. Only one finished the race, in 12th place, but a Grey Flash supplied to Vincent apprentice and future world champion John Surtees put up valiant short circuit performances.

Claimed to develop 35PS, the all-alloy engine has pushrod valve operation, with high-lift cams set high in the timing case to keep the rods short to maintain rigidity. Carburation is by an Amal TT instrument and ignition by a BTH magneto. A chain takes primary drive to a multi-plate clutch and four-speed gearbox supplied to Vincent by the Albion company.

The most radical aspect of the Vincent is its lightweight chassis, on similar lines to that of the company's V-twins. Devoid of a main tubular structure it uses the engine as a stressed member. A steel box-section beam containing engine oil supports the steering head at its front and provides a suspension unit anchor point at its rear. The cylinder head is supported near the front of the beam, while a vertical cast aluminium strut bolted near its rear end supports the gearbox.

The dual front brakes feature finned drums and backplates made in magnesium alloy and fitted with inlet and outlet air vents.

Unusual for its time, Vincent's rear suspension layout was a precursor of the monoshock system widely adopted in grand prix racing during the 1970s. The rear wheel is supported by a pivoted tubular subframe, which acts against two springs flanking a damper unit. At the front is Vincent's unusual Girdraulic fork, combining the parallel link principle of the tubular girder type with hydraulic damping. The main members are alloy forgings acting against enclosed coil springs in separate boxes, while a single damper unit is mounted centrally ahead of the steering stem.

▲ Vincent's cantilevered rear suspension predates monoshock types widely adopted on GP machines in the 1970s. The pivoted seat rises and falls with the unsprung subframe.

▼ Gear-driven cams placed high in the timing chest operate two valves via short, widely splayed pushrods and forked rockers engaging with the valve stems.

Engine type: Single-cylinder, air-cooled, pushrod two-valve four-stroke
Capacity: 499cc
Bore and stroke: 84mm x 90mm
Compression ratio: 8:1
Peak power: 35PS @ 6,200rpm
Fuel system: Amal TT carburettor
Gearbox: Four-speed
Suspension: Front, Girdraulic fork. Rear, sprung and damped cantilever
Brakes: Drums front and rear
Dry weight: 150kg
Top speed: 110mph

MINIMAL FRAME
With the power unit employed as a stressed member, normal frame tubing is absent on the Vincent. and magnesium components are used to cut weight.. Though promising, the Grey Flash made no real impact on the GP scene.

DKW THREE
349cc · 1953

Two-stroke engines were a minority choice for GP racing in the 1950s, and then almost exclusively entered only in the 125 and 250cc classes. But a notable exception was the highly innovative three-cylinder 350 fielded by the DKW factory, which had relocated westwards from Zschopau to Ingoldstat following the partition of Germany.

The DKW's three air-cooled cylinders, two slightly inclined from the vertical and the third disposed horizontally at 70 degrees to them, share a single crankshaft with big-end journals spaced at 120 degrees. Induction is by three 28mm Dell' Orto carburettors and piston-port intakes rather than the crankshaft driven rotary valves seen on earlier DKWs are used to avoid excessive engine width.

A Bosch magneto driven by bevel gears provides ignition sparks, while the exhaust system features crude expansion chambers that were refined to set a pattern for racing two-stroke systems adopted by other marques in later years

Swift, light and extremely noisy, the early version of the triple was let down by poor handling and unreliability. But DKW's racing chief Helmut Görg thoroughly reworked the design to make it more durable and highly competitive, eventually producing 46PS.

Direct oiling and coil ignition were adopted and the telescopic front fork replaced by a sturdier leading-link type. DKW adopted a sophisticated four-drum hydraulic braking system with proportionally-linked front and rear operation. On a machine that could hit 140mph when fitted with extensive streamlining designed at Munich Technical College, effective stopping was important, especially since a two-stroke does not produce an engine braking effect when the throttles are shut going into a corner.

Though never a GP winner, by 1955 the improved 'Deek' was a serious threat to Moto Guzzi's highly-developed four-stroke singles and German 350 champion August Höbl finished second to them in two GPs. He was runner-up in the 1956 350cc world championship but then, on the brink of glory, the DKW marque decided to withdraw from GP racing. The V3 two-stroke format was revived by Honda on its NS500 GP machine of 1983.

▲ A prominent feature of the two-stroke is the capacious alloy tank needed to deal with heavy fuel consumption. DKW used four sizes of tank, the largest holding 32 litres.

▼ Extremely compact, the air-cooled power unit incorporates a five-speed gearbox to cope with a narrow power band. The magneto was replaced by coil ignition during 1954.

Engine type: Three-cylinder, air-cooled, piston port two-stroke
Capacity: 349cc
Compression ratio: 12:1
Bore and stroke: 53mm x 52.8mm
Fuel system: Three 28mm Dell' Orto carburettors
Power: 46PS @ 9500rpm
Gearbox: Five-speed
Suspension: Front, telescopic fork. Rear, swingarm with twin shocks
Brakes: Drums front and rear
Dry weight: 145kg
Top speed: 140mph

TRIPLE AHEAD OF ITS TIME
The fast-accelerating three-cylinder 350cc DKW of the mid-1950s represented a giant leap forward for grand prix two-stroke technology. It would be ten years before two-strokes equalled its success in the 350 GP class.

NSU RENNMAX

247cc · 1953

Germany was only re-admitted to the FIM world championships at the end of 1951, but within two years, NSU's devastating 250cc Rennmax (renn means race) had achieved complete mastery of its class. Based on a doubling-up of the 125cc Rennfox power unit, its combined engine and gearbox has a similar look to the pre-war NSU twins, with inclined cylinders and double overhead camshafts. From 1953, it was slung from a spine-type frame fabricated in pressed steel.

With 'square' 54 x 54mm cylinder dimensions, the high-revving NSU unit designed by Walter Froede was developed to make 31PS at 10,400rpm. Camshaft drive is by a mix of spur and bevel gears, with a pair of splayed shafts on the right of the cylinders. Drive to the four speed gearbox is by chain and the lubrication system is supplied from a wet sump. Carburation is by two Amal remote-needle instruments and a battery-fed coil ignition system is used, rather than a magneto.

A short leading-link front fork was adopted for 1953, rear suspension being by a fabricated swingarm and twin shock absorbers. Aerodynamics, which were becoming increasingly important at the time, are improved by a small aluminium fairing and an extensive wheel-hugging front mudguard.

In 1953, the NSU Rennmax shook the GP world by winning four out of seven hard-fought 250cc GPs and factory rider Werner Haas became the first German rider to win a world championship. Haas and the newly-prominent marque also lifted the 1953 125cc title.

Rather than resting on its laurels, the company redesigned the Rennmax for 1954, providing it with a shorter stroke for higher rpm, a gear-driven six speed gearbox and rearranging the cam drive to employ a single shaft on the left of the cylinders. Producing 33bhp, NSU's 1954 works 250 was raced with more comprehensive streamlining and totally dominated the GPs that year to give Haas victory in five out of seven rounds and a convincing second world title.

When his team mate Rupert Hollaus was killed during practice for the final Italian round at Monza, NSU withdrew from the event and subsequently disbanded its extremely successful factory GP team.

▲ The inclined twin cylinder double overhead camshaft engine is slung from a novel spine frame fabricated from steel pressings. The exposed multiplate clutch runs dry.

▼ Leading-link front suspension maintains a constant wheelbase and provides lateral strength. A linkage attaches to the drum front brake's floating backplate.

Engine type: Parallel twin, air-cooled, double-overhead-camshaft, two-valve four-stroke
Capacity: 247cc
Bore and stroke: 54mm x 54mm
Compression ratio: 9.8:1
Fuel system: Two 25mm Amal carburettors
Power: 31PS @ 10,400rpm
Gearbox: Four-speed
Suspension: Front, leading-link fork. Rear, swingarm with twin shocks
Brakes: Drums front and rear
Dry weight: 115kg
Top speed: 125mph

TOP OF THE CLASS
The high-revving Rennmax twin of 1953 deposed Moto Guzzi's single as the top GP 250 and paved the way for even faster machinery that stormed the class again in 1954.

BMW RS54 RENNSPORT

492cc · 1954

BMW returned to the international GP racing arena in the early 1950s, sticking with the company's usual flat twin engine and shaft final drive, but developing an all-new 500 to replace ageing racers based on the supercharged pre-war type.

First aired as a works machine in 1953, the new double overhead camshaft twin devised by Alex von Falkenhausen was then marketed as the RS54 Rennsport model. Twenty solo machines and four sidecar outfits were snapped up for 1954 before they had even been built.

Housed in a tubular double cradle frame with swingarm rear suspension, the RS54 power unit is admirably compact for a horizontally-opposed twin. The crankshaft is made as short as possible, both to reduce engine length and minimise out-of-balance forces created by cylinders that are staggered to suit side-by-side big-ends.

Camshaft drive is by a shaft and bevel gears on each cylinder, linked by a short shaft to timing gears at the front of the engine. To avoid excessively wide cylinder heads, the close-coupled twin camshafts operate via rockers. An engine-speed clutch takes drive to the in-line four speed gearbox and the final drive shaft is incorporated in one side of the rear suspension's swingarm. The Rennsport was supplied both with a telescopic front fork and an Earles patent long leading link fork.

Works BMWs were advanced in using fuel injection on the faster GP circuits, but the production Rennsport has twin carburettors. Ignition is by a magneto driven from the timing gears along with the pump for the wet sump lubrication system.

Although the shaft drive twin's torque reactions reputedly made it difficult to handle at competitive GP speed, factory rider Walter Zeller was runner-up in the 1956 500cc world championships, with a short-stroke engine producing 13PS more than the standard 45.

But it was in the Sidecar class that the tireless flat twin engine made a tremendous impact on GP racing. BMW-powered machinery dominated the class from 1954 until 1974, winning every world championship except two.

▲ Usually raced with a full or half fairing, the Rennsport has a short wheelbase and the cylinders are well placed for air cooling. This example has the Earles leading-link front fork.

▼ Compact valve gear design keeps the flat twin engine as narrow as possible, but works rider Walter Zeller grounded down the cam boxes in corners, nevertheless.

Engine type: Flat-twin, air-cooled, double-overhead-camshaft, two-valve four-stroke
Capacity: 492cc
Bore and stroke: 66mm x 72mm
Compression ratio: 8:1
Fuel system: Two 30mm Fischer-Amal carburettors
Power: 45PS @ 8,000rpm
Gearbox: Four-speed
Suspension: Front, leading-link fork. Rear, swingarm with twin shocks
Brakes: Drums front and rear
Dry weight: 132kg
Top speed: 130mph

LONG-RUNNING TWIN
Although the factory 500cc solo gained some good GP results, it was in sidecar outfits that the Rennsport engine excelled. The three-wheel application suited its wide, low profile and the unit proved robust in long races.

MV AGUSTA

125cc · 1954

The first of MV Agusta's 39 road racing world championships was won by the Italian factory's 125cc double overhead camshaft model in 1952. Originally fielded in 1950 to replace MV's early 125cc two-stroke racer, the single cylinder dohc four-stroke rose to prominence in the hands of British rider Cecil Sandford and was subsequently ridden to five world titles by Italian Carlo Ubbiali. Although pressed hard at various times by Ducati, Mondial, Morini, MZ and NSU, the MV remained a top 125 until being eclipsed by Honda twins in 1961.

It was fielded with a variety of frame and suspension layouts, and the remarkable engine was steadily developed. A distinctive feature of the high-revving motor is a T-shaped enclosure for the train of gears taking drive from the crankshaft to the camshafts.

A gearbox in unit with the engine originally contained four gears but by 1960, when engines revved to 12,500rpm, six and seven speed internals were used. Carburation is by a 25mm Dell' Orto racing instrument with a flexibly-mounted floatbowl.

Drive for the ignition magneto and the externally-mounted engine oil pump at the front of the crankcase by gears. Location of the oil tank for the dry sump lubrication varied: in this case it is placed behind the fuel tank.

In the early 1950s, MV experimented with the long leading-link front fork patented by British fabrications specialist Ernie Earles, brought in by factory rider Les Graham to assist the Italian company with chassis development. An advantage gained over the telescopic fork is that machine wheelbase remains constant regardless of suspension movement, but riders' preference for the orthodox fork saw the Earles fork disappear from the works MVs during the 1950s.

Handlebar fairings were superseded by complete front and rear enclosure for faster GP circuits, until the FIM banned full fairings after 1957 and a modern 'dolphin' fairing was adopted. In fully-faired form, a 125cc MV ridden by Ubbiali lapped the Belgian Spa Francorchamps GP course at 99.91mph (160. 79km/h) in 1956.

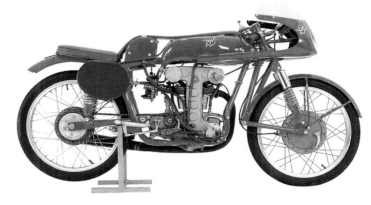

▲ A T-shaped cover contains the train of eight pinions taking drive from the crankshaft to the twin overhead camshafts. In its ultimate form the MV revved to 12,000rpm and made 20PS.

▼ Fabricated from lightweight steel tubing, the Earles leading-link front fork has easily-changed Girling oil-damped suspension units. Front brake drum diameter is 180mm.

Engine type: Single-cylinder, air-cooled, double-overhead-camshaft, two-valve four-stroke
Capacity: 125cc
Bore and stroke: 53mm x 56mm
Compression ratio: 9.5:1
Fuel system: 25mm Dell' Orto carburettor
Power: 13PS @ 10,000rpm
Gearbox: Four-speed
Suspension: Front, leading-link fork. Rear, swingarm with twin shocks
Brakes: Drums front and rear
Dry weight: 78kg
Top speed: 110mph

SOUND SINGLE
Winning 34 GP races and six world championships between 1952 and 1960 proved the basically sound design of MV Agusta's high-revving little single, but it was then eclipsed by a new generation of 125s.

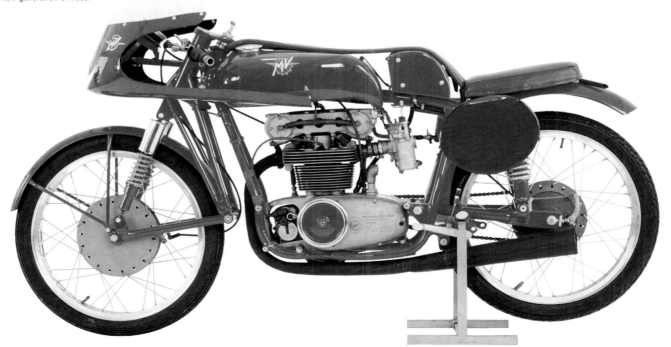

NSU RENNFOX

125cc · 1954

Like its bigger 250cc Rennmax counterpart, NSU's 125cc Rennfox owed much of its technical specification to experience with the company's promising 500cc R54 four-cylinder racer, which was abandoned after 1951 because NSU's commercial focus was to be on small capacity motorcycles.

First appearing during 1951, the 125cc engine had a single inclined cylinder with internal bore and stroke dimensions of 54 x 54mm. A single shaft and bevel drive distributed motion to the double overhead camshafts via spur gears. Like the 250, it was fitted in a pressed steel spine-type frame with a short leading-link front fork.

NSU overcame the dominant Mondials and MV Agustas to win the 1952 125cc German GP, but it was in 1953 and 1954 that NSU swept the board in both of the small capacity classes. Further development during the latter two seasons saw the Rennfox being wholly redesigned and acquiring a shorter stroke format. Dry sump lubrication replaced a wet sump and coil ignition was adopted instead of a magneto. At first, the revised engine had single overhead camshaft valve gear, but a dohc version soon appeared.

Considerable development work also went into devising ever more efficient streamlining and like the Rennmax, the Rennfox first acquired a dolphin-like aluminium fairing with a 'beak' projecting over the front wheel, and then full streamlining that enclosed the front wheel, employed on the fastest GP circuits where the 125 could reach 115mph.

To help slow the machine from high velocity a twin-leading-shoe drum front brake was adopted, incorporating a floating mechanism to suit the front suspension movement.

Factory rider Werner Haas won three out of six 125cc GPs to narrowly wrest the 1953 title from MV and in the following season his team mate Ruppert Hollaus won four out of six to take the championship posthumously after being killed in practice for the Italian GP.

NSU also demonstrated its technical prowess with a series of speed records during the 1950s, but the factory opted to withdraw its GP team while it was on top, to concentrate on commercial production.

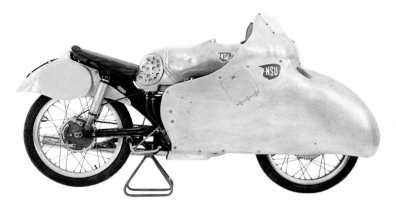

▲ A product of intense and methodical development, the 125cc NSU achieved clear superiority in its class before the German factory withdrew its GP squad after 1954.

▼ The development of efficient streamlining typified NSU's scientific approach to GP racing. With the 125 engine ultimately producing 18PS, maximum was 115mph.

Engine type: Single-cylinder, double-overhead-camshaft, two-valve four-stroke
Capacity: 125cc
Bore and stroke: 58mm x 47.3mm
Compression ratio: 9.8:1
Fuel system: 30mm Amal carburettor
Power: 18PS @ 11,500rpm
Gearbox: Six-speed
Brakes: Drums front and rear
Suspension: Front, Short leading-link fork. Rear, swingarm with twin shock absorbers
Dry weight: 85kg
Top speed: 115mph (with full fairing)

SHAPED FOR SPEED
A cutaway sculpted into the aluminium fuel tank accommodates the steeply-downdraughted carburettor. The exhaust pipe tapers gently, terminating in a reverse cone.

GILERA SATURNO

499cc · 1955

Most renowned for its world-beating four cylinder racers, the Gilera company of Arcore in Northern Italy also created the 500cc single cylinder Saturno. Produced as a suitable machine for privateers, the limited-edition racing version of the Saturno roadster was also chosen as a mount for factory riders at particular events, especially on tight circuits where top speed was not at a premium.

Designed by Giuseppe Salmaggi and named after a Roman god, the Saturno was first launched for 1940, but Italy's entry to World War II caused production to be suspended until 1946 when updated road and competition versions appeared. In subsequent years engine and chassis development refined the Saturno and the final Corsa racer produced from 1952 to 1957 was nicknamed the Piuma (feather), because of its light weight and easy handling.

Although it was considerably updated during its production life, the Saturno engine is unsophisticated, not even employing an overhead camshaft. Based on a main casing containing the crankcase, gearbox and wet sump lubrication system, the long-stroke unit has two valves operated by pushrods and rockers from a gear driven camshaft in the timing chest.

Carburation is by a single Dell' Orto instrument, while ignition sparks are generated by a Marelli magneto sited at the front of the engine, driven by pinions from the camshaft gear train. The enclosed primary drive is by gears, with the final drive chain situated on the right side of the machine. Selection of the four gearbox ratios is by a rocking pedal.

The tubular frame is open-bottomed, with a single downtube supporting the front of the engine unit, and suspension is conventional for its time, with a telescopic front fork and a tubular swingarm with twin shock absorbers at the rear. Various drum front brakes were fitted, including the large diameter type fitted to contemporary factory fours and the example shown here wears a full fairing similar to that seen on the 1955 multi.

Light, and more agile than its appearance would suggest, the lively Saturno was viewed with afffection by those who raced it.

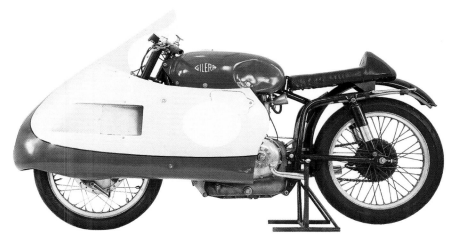

▲ Brisk acceleration and agile handling on short, twisty circuits were the Saturno's strong points. The 500cc singles had their own dedicated race shop in the Gilera factory.

▼ A 'dustbin' fairing lifts the top speed of moderately powered single to 130mph. Full streamlining that enveloped the front wheel was banned by FIM rules after 1957.

Engine type: Single-cylinder, air-cooled, pushrod, two-valve four-stroke
Capacity: 499cc
Bore and stroke: 84mm x 90mm
Compression ratio: 8:1
Fuel system: 38mm Dell' Orto carburettor
Power: 42PS @ 6,500rpm
Gearbox: Four-speed
Suspension: Front, telescopic fork. Rear, swingarm with twin shocks
Brakes: Drums front and rear
Dry weight: 175kg
Top speed: 130mph (with fairing)

ITALIAN PRIVATEER
An earlier version of the Saturno won the 1948 Italian Grand Prix ridden by Arciso Artesiani, but in the world championships the single was an Italian equivalent of the Manx Norton in providing a mount for privateers.

MATCHLESS G45

498cc · 1955

Sold by AMC in tandem with the 350cc AJS 7R from 1953 to 1957, the Matchless G45 was aimed at 500cc class privateers. First seen as a factory prototype which took an easy win at the 1952 Senior Manx GP with Derek Farrant on board, it was powered by a parallel twin pushrod engine based on that of the Matchless G9 roadster.

When the G45 first became available in small numbers for the 1953 season, riders were impressed by its speed and handling, but less happy with vibration, poor reliability and oil leaks. Even the AMC factory team, which campaigned G45s alongside its more exotic 500cc E95 Porcupine twin, struck countless troubles. For 1959, AMC enlarged the more successful ohc 350cc 7R single to create the Matchless G50, which proved more competitive than the G45 against the rival Manx Norton.

Clear external differences from the roadgoing Matchless G9 engine are the all-alloy construction and finning on the exhaust-side rocker boxes. The 360-degree crankshaft is supported in three main bearings, the central one being a plain shell type supported by a plate in the vertically-split crankcase. Early G45s had a machined-billet steel crank, but production machines were fitted with a forged type. The pushrods and rockers are activated by two gear-driven camshafts in the upper crankcase and the same train of gears turns a Lucas SRR2 ignition magneto behind the cylinders.

Carburation was originally by a pair of Amal TTs, although the example shown has later Concentrics. A remote oil tank supplies the dry sump lubrication system, which has gear-driven feed and scavenge pumps sited in the timing chest. Primary drive to the Burman four-speed gearbox is by chain.

The frame is of similar layout to the 7R, with AMC's own telescopic front fork and substantial rear shock absorbers with clevis fixings to the frame and swinging arm. The G45's effective twin-leading-shoe 203mm drum front brake was originally developed for AMC's factory race team and features air ducting on the magnesium alloy backplate to scoop cool air in at the front and release heated air rearwards. For cleaner running at low rpm, plain exhaust megaphones were replaced by reverse cones during production.

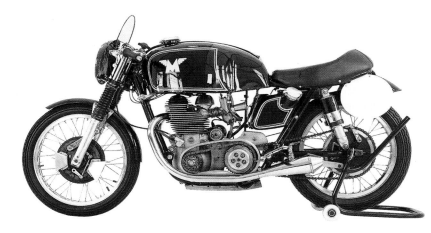

▲ The twin exhaust pipes terminate in megaphones with reverse-cone outlets to boost mid-range performance. Chubby rear suspension units are AMC's own.

▼ A sound handler with powerful brakes, the rasping Matchless parallel twin was audibly distinguishable from its single and four cylinder track rivals.

Engine type: Parallel twin, air cooled, pushrod, two-valve four-stroke
Capacity: 498cc
Bore and stroke: 66mm x 72mm
Compression ratio: 9.5:1
Fuel system: Two 28mm Amal TT carburettors
Power: 48PS @ 7,200rpm
Gearbox: Four-speed
Suspension: Front, telescopic fork. Rear, swingarm with twin shocks
Brakes: Drums front and rear
Dry weight: 145kg
Top speed: 125mph

SHAKER AND BREAKER
It was AMC management's preferred policy to race machines related to production roadsters, but while the G45's twin cylinder pushrod engine produced enough power, it suffered from vibration and unreliability.

NSU SPORTMAX 251RS

247cc · 1955

In 1954, the Grand Prix world was shocked when reigning 125 and 250cc world champion make NSU announced the withdrawal of its works teams. But the marque did not disappear completely from the GPs, as its race shop had developed the Sportmax 251RS based on the 250cc single-overhead cam Max roadster, and made it available to privateers in limited numbers. Although resembling the single cylinder Max unit, the engine offered much more performance, with a top speed of over 120mph in streamlined form.

Like the road engine, the Sportmax features an unusual form of camshaft drive devised by NSU engineer Albert Roder. Called the Ultramax system by NSU, it uses eccentric driving wheels and connecting rods driven off the left of the crankshaft via a half-time pinion. Rockers bearing on the single camshaft actuate two valves, against the readily replaced hairpin type valve springs still commonly used on racing engines of the 1950s.

The pressed-steel beam frame with swingarm rear suspension is similar to that of the works Rennmax. Its front fork is a short leading-link fork with strong fabricated legs, each containing a spring and damper unit to control the movement of the links supporting the wheel spindle. One advantage of this design is its lack of dive under heavy braking, which is provided at the front wheel by a substantial 210mm drum.

Fashioned in sheet aluminium, the full fairing fitted to factory supported machines is a work of art. It has intakes for cooling air and the screen is set within the upper section. Complementing the enclosure is a shapely fuel tank with 22 litre capacity.

Proof of the NSU's competitiveness came when it was ridden to the 1955 250cc world championship by veteran racer Hermann-Peter Müller. He narrowly beat MV Agusta rider Bill Lomas, who had amassed equal points but had been penalised for a rule infringement at the Dutch GP.

Sammy Miller, Tommy Robb and John Surtees were among the up-and-coming stars who reaped good results in GPs and other major races with the limited-issue Sportmax. Even when no longer a GP front runner, the NSU raced on for another decade.

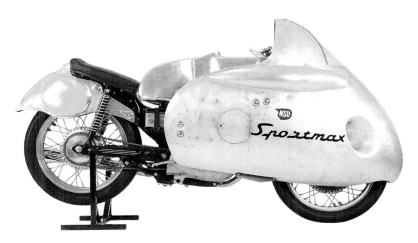

▲ The tuned single cylinder engine, pressed-steel spine frame, effective brakes and streamlining combined to make the Sportmax into a highly efficient machine capable of GP success.

▼ Based on works team experience, the massive aluminium fairing boosted the 28PS single's maximum speed to 125mph. Bulges on the sides are to clear the rider's hands.

Engine type: Single-cylinder, air-cooled, single-overhead-camshaft, two-valve four-stroke
Capacity: 247cc
Bore and stroke: 69mm x 66mm
Compression ratio: 9.8:1
Fuel system: 30mm Amal carburettor
Power: 28PS @ 9,000rpm
Gearbox: Four-speed
Suspension: Front, short leading-link fork. Rear, swingarm with twin shocks
Brakes: Drums front and rear
Dry weight: 115kg
Top speed: 125mph

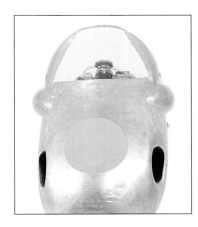

EXCLUSIVE WEAPON
Very expensive and only available to racers with the requisite contacts, NSU's Sportmax was the best 250cc mount that a non-works GP rider could wish for in the late 1950s.

MOTO GUZZI

349cc · 1956

From 1953 to 1957, Moto Guzzi reigned over the 350cc world championships with a run of 24 GP victories resulting in five titles. They were won with single-cylinder dohc machines directly descended from the Italian factory's pre-war sohc 250, using a blend of fine handling, ultra-lightweight construction and aerodynamics rather than sheer power output.

The man behind the phenomenal olive green singles was Giulio Carcano, whose creative brilliance was also to be applied to bob sleighs and yachts for Italy's national teams. He undertook a programme of continuous experimentation and refinement to keep the simple boosted 250s competitive against Gilera and MV's 350cc fours and DKW's two-stroke triple. The Guzzi engine was raced in 310, 320 and 345cc versions before the full 350 size was perfected from 1954.

Carcano's design ideas included plating the alloy cylinder's bore to dispense with the weight of an iron liner while enhancing heat dispersion and a short leading-link front fork giving true steering plus an anti-dive effect under braking. He also employed Guzzi's wind tunnel to develop highly efficient fairings and his 1954 projectile featured a comprehensive space-frame and a fuel tank mounted below seat level.

The machine seen here is of a type fielded in 1956, using a more conventional frame. Hidden beneath the fuel tank, its main member is a large diameter spinal tube running from the steering head to the front of the seat. The front fork has discrete spring and damper struts to control the movement of the leading-links. A half fairing has replaced the original full type.

The engine follows Guzzi's classic horizontal cylinder layout with a long, downdraughted carburettor tract and a crankshaft flywheel mounted externally, outboard of the geared primary drive to an enclosed clutch and five-speed gearbox. Ignition is by magneto: Carcano also experimented with coil ignition, including dual systems firing twin plugs.

By 1957 it was becoming increasingly hard to defeat the fours, but if Guzzi had not retired from the GPs it is likely that Carcano would have fielded a 350cc version of his amazing 500cc V8.

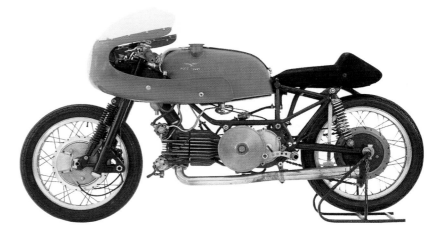

▲ The flat single layout keeps weight usefully low for superior handling. The external flywheel, seen on Guzzi engines since the 1920s, smoothes out power impulses.

▼ The preserved 1956 350 in action at the 1998 Assen historic festival. Light weight helps the Guzzi accelerate better and shortens braking distances.

Engine type: Single-cylinder, double overhead camshaft, two-valve four-stroke
Capacity: 349cc
Bore and stroke: 80mm x 69.5mm
Compression ratio: 9.8:1
Fuel system: 35mm Dell' Orto carburettor
Power: 35PS @ 7,800rpm
Gearbox: Five-speed
Suspension: Front: short leading-link fork. Rear, swingarm with twin shocks
Brakes: Drums front and rear
Dry weight: 106kg
Top speed: 135mph (with full fairing)

SOPHISTICATED SINGLE
A simple and sturdy engine, strong triangulated frame and powerful drum brakes add up to a highly competitive package, able to reach 135mph with a full fairing.

GILERA FOUR

500CC · 1957

Gilera dominated 500cc grand prix racing from 1950 to 1957. In those eight seasons, the marque based at Arcore in Northern Italy won 31 GPs and six world titles in the premier capacity class. The bellowing red and white Gileras were sometimes beaten, but their overall supremacy was clear.

The factory had fielded a successful supercharged 500cc liquid-cooled four of external design prior to World War II. But the postwar 500 engine was based on a blown air-cooled 250 four drawn up in-house by Piero Remor for 1940, revised to be eligible for world championship racing. Remor defected to the rival MV Agusta factory in 1949, but his successor Franco Passoni developed the Gilera four into its ultimate, all-conquering form. He was aided by British world champion Geoff Duke, who left Norton to join the Italian team in 1953.

Gilera's double overhead camshaft transverse four with inclined cylinders set the definitive pattern for high-revving four-stroke racing engines. Drive to the cams is by a train of gears from the centre of the crankshaft, gears also being used to drive the integral five-speed gearbox. Engine oil is carried in a wet sump, finned on its exterior to aid cooling. A Lucas rotating magnet magneto mounts behind the cylinders, supplying sparks to central plugs.

Duke helped develop the chassis along Norton lines, to make the machine sleeker, lower and easier to handle. The telescopic fork is strongly braced in the region of the top yokes and rear suspension is by a swingarm with twin shock absorbers. Both 200mm drum brakes have twin-leading-shoe operation. Though rather heavy, a 48PS 350cc version also scored some successes from 1955-1957.

From 1955, full 'dustbin' streamlining was fitted for faster circuits, while the team reverted to a brief half fairing for short tracks, or in windy conditions.

One of the 500cc Gilera's many fine achievements was when Scots rider Bob McIntyre recorded the first 100mph laps of the TT Course in winning the 1957 Senior event. That year's 500cc world title went to Italian teamster Libero Liberati but at the end of the 1957 season Gilera, along with Moto Guzzi and Mondial, withdrew from GP racing.

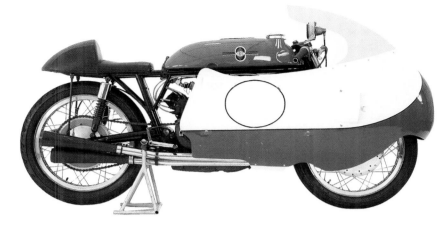

▲ The ignition magneto can be seen below the rear portion of the fuel tank. A long stretch from the clip-on handlebars to the seat reflects the riding style of the time.

▼ Inclined cylinders, distinctive camboxes, centrally located spark plugs and a ribbed crankcase venting tube are clearly visible on the Gilera when fitted with a half fairing.

Engine type: Four-cylinder, air-cooled, double-overhead-camshaft, two-valve four-stroke
Capacity: 500cc
Bore and stroke: 52mm x 58.8mm
Compression ratio: 9.8:1
Fuel system: Four 32mm Dell' Orto carbs
Power: 66PS @ 10, 500rpm
Gearbox: Five-speeds
Suspension: Front, telescopic fork. Rear, swingarm with twin shocks
Brakes: Drums front and rear
Dry weight: 140kg
Top speed: 150mph

DEFINITIVE FOUR
The ultimate grand prix machine of its era. The growling 500cc Gilera four was potent and aerodynamic, with sound roadholding and effective brakes. The marque won six 500cc titles between 1950 and 1957.

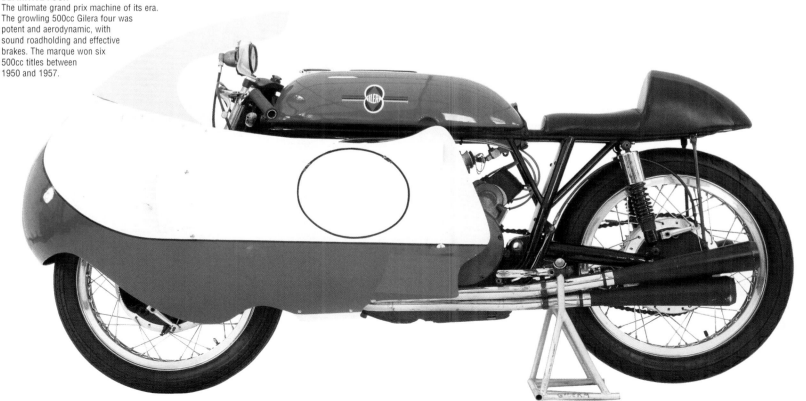

MOTO GUZZI V8

499cc · 1957

Moto Guzzi wheeled out the most technically exciting machine ever seen on a GP grid for its first race in 1956. Aiming to depose Gilera and MV Agusta fours as kings of the 500cc class, Guzzi's V8 was an intricate masterpiece executed by the factory's brilliant designer Giulio Carcano.

While his light, sure-handling single-cylinder machine topped the 350cc category, Carcano knew that only sheer power could ultimately beat the fours. Guzzi had raced a slim-line 500cc longitudinal shaft-driven four (which had been designed outside the factory) during 1953 and 1954, but the engine's torque reactions created handling quirks.

Carcano looked to a multiplicity of cylinders as a way of achieving high rpm and efficient power production, while keeping frontal area to a minimum. He set two banks of four cylinders on a single transverse crankshaft at a vee angle of 90 degrees. Eight tiny carburettors were packed inside the vee and drive to the double overhead camshafts was by gears on the right side of the unit, where a pump for the liquid cooling system was also located. Gears took primary drive to a gearbox with four-, five- and six-speed options.

Chassis design followed the normal Guzzi pattern of the time. The tubular frame had a large diameter top tube doubling up as the oil tank and the front fork featured a short leading-link. Rear suspension was by a conventional tubular swingarm with twin shocks.

Using the 1956 season for development, Carcano's team began to see results in the following year when the humming V8 won a major Italian national event, and finished fourth in the 302-mile Isle of Man TT despite a holed piston. Wearing a full fairing, the Guzzi was timed at 178mph in the Belgian GP, making it the fastest GP racer ever. By the end of 1957, the engine was producing 80PS, a figure that was not matched by a unblown GP 500 until the 1970s. And the whole machine weighed only 136kg.

Unfortunately, the V8's promising career was cut short by Moto Guzzi's commercial decision to pull out of GP racing after 1957. Carcano had a new, improved 500 engine and an intriguing 350 version of the V8 on the stocks for 1958, but both had to be abandoned.

▲ With a full fairing less than 60cm wide, the Guzzi could reach speed in excess of 175mph on the faster GP circuits. Scoops supply air to the cooling system's low-slung radiator.

▼ The gear train driving the dohc valve gear is in a large magnesium casing, with the water pump in the centre. Removing the tank reveals the large-diameter oil-bearing frame top tube.

Engine type: V8, liquid-cooled, dohc two-valve four-stroke
Capacity: 499cc
Bore and stroke: 44 x 41mm
Compression ratio: 11:1
Fuel system: Eight 21mm Dell' Ortos
Power: 80PS @ 13,000rpm
Gearbox: Five-speed (with other options)
Suspension: Front: leading-link front fork. Rear, swingarm with twin shock absorbers
Brakes: Drums front and rear
Dry weight: 136kg
Top speed: 178mph

PRODIGIOUS POTENTIAL
By 1957 Giulio Carcano's astonishing V8 was producing 80PS and handling well, despite the crude tyres of the time. Sadly, this fascinating line of development was cut short by Guzzi's decision to disband its GP team.

MOTO MORINI

247cc · 1958

Although Moto Morini never won a world championship, the Bologna factory had the distinction of developing the ultimate single cylinder four-stroke GP machine. Ridden by Tarquinio Provini, Morini's phenomenally fast 250 beat Honda fours in several 1963 GPs and only narrowly failed to take that year's world title when its rider had to contest the final Japanese round while suffering from an ear infection.

The company, set up by Alfonso Morini after he split off from the MM marque just prior to World War Two, contested the inaugural 1949 world championship with a 125cc two-stroke. That was rapidly replaced by a single overhead camshaft four-stroke for 1950 but with no GP wins scored, Morini withdrew two years later to concentrate on production machine-oriented Italian national racing.

The marque reappeared on the international scene in 1957, when Morini entered the Italian GP with a double overhead camshaft 250cc single based on its 175cc sohc Rebello, which had been successful in Italy's long-distance public roads races. Racing against highly-developed Mondial, MV Agusta and Moto Guzzi singles, Morini's rider Emilio Mendogni held third position for much of the race before retiring.

Like the Rebello, the GP racer based on it has an inclined cylinder and camshaft drive by chain, but with two camshafts in place of one. Gears take drive to the ignition magneto, located behind the cylinder above the five-speed gearbox and primary drive is also by gears. Oil for the dry sump lubrication system is carried in a tank under the seat.

The open-bottomed tubular frame has a single downtube, flanked on the machine shown here by bracing strips. An Amadoro double-sided drum provides braking power at the front, backed up by a single rear drum.

This interim model was replaced late in 1958 by a new upright 250cc dohc single with gear driven camshafts. At that year's Italian GP, Mendogni and Gianpiero Zubani took first and second places ahead of Carlo Ubbiali's MV Agusta. It was this revised machine that was developed into the legendary Honda-beating single ridden by Provini.

▲ Still bearing a similarity to the Rebello sports racer, the 1957-1958 Morini has an inclined cylinder, twin overhead camshafts, hairpin valve springs and magneto ignition.

▼ An oil feed line to the valve gear runs up the outside of the camshaft drive chain cover. Carburation is by a 30mm Dell' Orto with a flexibly mounted remote floatbowl.

Engine type: Single-cylinder, air-cooled, double-overhead-camshaft, two-valve four-stroke
Capacity: 247cc
Bore and stroke: 69mm x 66mm
Compression ratio: 9:1
Fuel system: 30mm Dell' Orto carburettor
Power: 29PS @ 10,000rpm
Gearbox: Five-speed
Suspension: Front, telescopic fork. Rear, swingarm with twin shocks
Brakes: Drums front and rear
Dry weight: 113kg
Top speed: 125mph (with fairing)

EVOLVING SINGLE
A halfway stage between Morini's 175cc long-distance racer and the devastatingly fast 250cc single of the early 1960s, the Rebello-based machine had a claimed 29PS, putting it on a par with Mondial's title-winning 250.

MV AGUSTA SIX

499cc · 1958

Intense rivalry between the major Italian GP contenders in the mid 1950s made for rapid technical progress. In the 500cc class, the Gilera four's grip on the world championships was challenged by MV Agusta's similar four. MV took over the title in 1956, albeit after a troubled season for Gilera when works riders Geoff Duke and Reg Armstrong missed some GP rounds, having been suspended by the FIM for expressing support for privateers in a start money dispute at Assen in 1955.

Gilera and MV also faced a threat from Moto Guzzi, a company which had been concentrating on the smaller classes but astonished the world by unveiling its 500cc liquid-cooled V8 in 1955. Count Agusta's company responded by building its own piece of super-exotica, with six cylinders.

Retaining the in-line air-cooled format of its fast-improving 500cc four, the six joined MV's line-up for the 1957 Italian GP but was only used for practice. Then, at the end of the season Gilera, Mondial and Moto Guzzi decided to stop pouring money into GP competition and concentrate on commercial realities. These companies believed that MV would join them, but Agusta's factory, which manufactured helicopters as well as motorcycles, continued to contest GPs.

With only BMW providing serious opposition in the 500cc class, MV shelved the six without any further development. It did race once, however, in the 1958 Italian GP, when John Hartle retired with machine problems after duelling with Walter Zeller's BMW. He reported that it only ran at slightly higher rpm than MV's 10,500rpm four but had a noticeably narrower power band. The machine was then all but forgotten until a group of Italian MV enthusiasts restored it in the late 1980s to make demo appearances at major historic racing events.

With slightly 'over-square' 48 x 46mm bore and stroke dimensions, the prototype engine has been kept as narrow as possible and is housed, along with a five-speed gearbox, in a tubular double-cradle frame similar to the four's. The prototype was originally tested with a full fairing of the type outlawed by the FIM after 1957.

▲ The front brake is a double-sided twin-leading-shoe drum and the front fork has spindle mounts set ahead of the sliders. Engine layout resembles that of MV's fours.

▼ The first GP machine to sport six exhaust megaphones. Lack of 500cc opposition after 1957 meant that the MV's stirring sound was only heard in one race, the 1958 Italian GP.

Engine type: In-line six cylinder, air cooled, double-overhead-camshaft, two-valve four-stroke
Capacity: 499cc
Bore and stroke: 48mm x 46mm
Compression ratio: 10.8:1
Fuel system: Six 26mm Dell' Orto carbs
Power: 75PS @ 10,800rpm
Gearbox: Six-speed
Suspension: Front, telescopic fork. Rear, swingarm with twin shocks
Brakes: Drums front and rear
Dry weight: 145kg
Top speed: 150mph

GP RACING'S FIRST SIX
The six Dell' Orto carburettors have slim 'matchbox' float chambers and ignition is by magneto. Further development might have produced a better power gain over the 500cc four than the 5PS increase quoted.

BENELLI
248cc · 1959

▲ Sweeping between the frame downtubes, the exhaust pipe has a long, gently tapered megaphone. Hairpin-type springs are used to close the two valves.

B ased in Pesaro, Italy, the company founded in 1911 by the six Benelli brothers scored its first international successes in the 1920s. By the mid-1930s Benelli had developed a 250cc single with double overhead camshafts and this influential design brought the factory TT glory in 1939 when Irish rider Ted Mellors outpaced stiff opposition to win the Lightweight event.

When the world championships were instituted in 1949, Benelli was prominent in the 250cc class with updated singles that set a scorching pace. Factory rider Dario Abrosini was runner-up that year and romped the championship in 1950, winning three out of four GPs, including the TT. But his fatal accident at the French round when leading the championship on a redesigned single in the next year was followed by a period of GP inactivity for Benelli.

The still-small marque returned in 1959 with an updated 250cc short-stroke single, ridden in GPs by Dickie Dale, rising Italian star Silvio Grassetti and former world champion Geoff Duke. But despite a claimed 33PS at 10,500rpm the Benelli was outpaced by the more consistently developed machinery of MV and MZ. Then in 1960, the arrival of Honda's four-cylinder 250s made life really tough for a quarter-litre four-stroke single.

Benelli responded with its own four, but failed to have one ready for Mike Hailwood to ride in the 1962 Lightweight TT. He rode a privately-owned ex-works single instead, and held it in a creditable fourth spot behind Honda fours before its engine blew under the strain.

Exhibiting classical Italian architecture, the 70 x 64.8mm engine has twin overhead camshafts driven by a train of pinions in a casing on the right side of the cylinder. One of the gears is used to operate contact breaker points for the battery and coil ignition. Primary drive is by gears, to a dry clutch and a six-speed gearbox. The power unit is extremely compact, helping to achieve a short wheelbase for cornering agility. The frame is a simple tubular type with a single top tube and twin downtubes continuing under the engine. Oil for the dry sump lubrication system is stored in a tank below the seat.

▼ The tidy power unit has a breather vent behind the cylinder, alongside the Dell' Orto carburettor. A linkage is used for the gearchange, sited on the right side.

Engine: Single-cylinder, air-cooled, double-overhead-camshaft, two-valve four-stroke
Capacity: 248cc
Bore and stroke: 70mm x 64.8mm
Compression ratio: 11.5:1
Fuel system: 30mm Dell 'Orto carburettors
Power: 33PS @ 11,500rpm
Gearbox: Six-speed
Suspension: Front, telescopic fork. Rear, swingarm with twin shocks
Brakes: Drums front and rear
Dry weight: n/a
Top speed: 125mph

BEHIND THE GAME
Appearing after Benelli had missed several GP seasons, the 250cc single evolved from the company's extremely competitive early 1950s' machine but was no match for the latest high-revving fours and two-strokes.

JAWA

248cc · 1959

The Czechoslovakian Jawa company joined the GP circus in the mid-1950s, by which time it had already developed solid and sophisticated machines to race in home and non-championship international events. The Jawas were powered by twin cylinder engines with shaft and bevel-driven double overhead camshafts and fielded in 250, 350 and 500cc versions. Their tubular chassis were conventional for the time, although Jawa did experiment with small 16-inch diameter wheels, which were to enjoy popularity for front fitment on GP machines many years later in the early 1980s.

It was the next generation of Jawas that would make a good showing in 1960 GPs, most notably in the 350cc class. The revised parallel twin engine was first seen on the 250 of the late 1950s. Rather than having its camshaft drive shaft sited on the right side of the slightly inclined cylinders, it was now placed centrally behind them and driven from a jackshaft. The vertical shaft turned the rearmost inlet camshaft via bevel gears and drive was then taken forward to the exhaust camshaft by a shaft placed horizontally across the top of the cylinder head.

To promote efficient combustion, each cylinder had twin spark plugs, powered by a battery and coil system and induction was by a pair of Amal GP carburettors with a remote floatbowl. Primary drive to a six-speed gearbox built in unit with the engine was by gears on the left side, where the dry clutch and its operating arm were easily accessible. The gearchange pedal was sited on the right. Where the earlier Jawa twins had dry sump lubrication, oil was now carried in the lower portion of the main engine casings.

Like several other makers, Jawa followed the pattern set by Norton in using a double cradle tubular frame. But this machine is unusual in the way that the swingarm pivots outboard of the main tubes, rather than inside them. British Girling rear suspension units are fitted, while at the front the telscopic fork has external coil springs.

Always progressive and imaginative, Jawa made extensive use of tough yet light glass-fibre mouldings for fuel tanks, seats and fairings at a time when many makers still relied on aluminium.

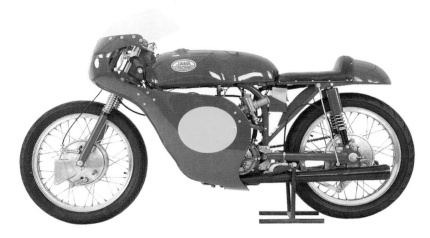

▲ The twin-leading-shoe drum front brake has a large scoop to collect cooling air. A battery carried under the seat nose powers the ignition system, via double-ended coils.

▼ The exposed dry multi-plate clutch is on the left of the power unit. The twin-spark ignition system uses pairs of plugs of 10mm, rather than the usual 13mm, size.

Engine type: Parallel twin, air-cooled, double-overhead-camshaft, four-valve four-stroke
Capacity: 248cc
Bore and stroke: 55mm x 52mm
Compression ratio: n/a
Fuel system: Two Amal GP carburettors
Power: 36PS @ 10,800rpm
Gearbox: Six-speed
Suspension: Front, Telescopic front fork. Rear, swingarm with twin shock absorbers
Brakes: Drums front and rear
Dry weight: 120kg
Top speed: 120mph

SOUND BASIS

Although rather bulky and heavy for a 250, the Jawa parallel twin of circa 1960 paved the way for a faster 350cc version of the same weight that was a regular GP podium finisher.

MV AGUSTA DESMODROMIC

125cc · 1959

Although MV Agusta was the predominant marque in the 125cc GP class after NSU's departure at the end of 1954, the Gallarate factory's dohc singles faced intense competition from its Italian rivals. Mondial wrested the 1957 title from MV with Drusiani's latest single and Gilera's twin-cylinder 125 contender had put Romolo Ferri second in the 1956 series behind MV maestro Carlo Ubbiali.

Moto Morini was a fading threat, but MV had a tough new opponent in the form of Ducati. The aspiring Bologna factory had set many speed records and enjoyed great success in Italian long-distance road races with a 100cc dohc single designed by Fabio Taglioni, who had left Mondial to join Ducati. A brilliant engineer, Taglioni developed a single incorporating desmodromic valve operation to contest the 125cc world championship.

This system had been experimented with since the earliest days of motor racing and was notably used in the Mercedes Benz car that won the 1954 Formula One championship. Rather than relying on springs to return poppet valves to their seats, a desmodromic mechanism uses cam profiles and rockers to positively close the valves as well as opening them. Its advantages are precise timings and enhanced gas sealing at very high rpm as well as the elimination of valve 'float', which can cause mechanical damage to valves and pistons.

By 1958, Taglioni's 125 'desmo' was able to eclipse MV in three GPs, won by works riders Alberto Gandossi and Bruno Spaggiari. And Ducati's sweep of the first five places in the Italian GP was said to have infuriated the proud Count Agusta.

Looking at every possible means of wringing more power from its 125 without sacrificing reliability, MV experimented with its own desmodromic engine. Based on the marque's existing dohc single, the prototype made only one competitive appearance in an Italian national championship race at Modena early in 1959. Ridden by factory rider Tarquinio Provini, the MV desmo strongly challenged the leading Ducati in heavy rain before retiring, never to be seen racing in anger again.

EXPERIMENTAL ENGINE
Clearly inspired by Ducati's dramatic GP success with a 125cc desmodromic engine, the MV only raced once before being shelved. Ubbiali's retirement at the end of 1960 marked MV's withdrawal from the 125 and 250cc GPs.

▲ As on MV's conventional dohc 125 single of the time, the desmodromic engine is carried in a double cradle frame with swingarm rear suspension and telescopic front fork.

▼ A train of gears takes drive from the crankshaft to the massive cam box containing the gears, cams and cam followers which operate the desmodromic valve gear.

Engine type: Single-cylinder, air-cooled, double-overhead-camshaft desmodromic, two-valve four-stroke
Capacity: 125cc
Bore and stroke: 53mm x 56mm
Compression ratio: 9.5:1
Fuel system: Dell' Orto carburettor
Power: 20PS @ 12,000rpm (estimated)
Gearbox: Six-speed
Suspension: Front, telescopic fork. Rear, swingarm with twin shocks
Brakes: Drums front and rear
Dry weight: n/a
Top speed: 112mph (estimated)

MZ

125cc · 1959

The foundations of modern GP two-stroke technology were laid by MZ and its brilliant engineer Walter Kaaden in the late 1950s and early 1960s. Despite the disadvantages of operating from Eastern Germany — MZ's Zschopau base was on the site of the pre-war DKW plant — Kaaden's team was a constant threat to Italy and Japan's best in the 125 and 250cc GP classes.

MZ burst onto the GP scene in 1958 with a victory in the 250cc Swedish GP. But winning the 125cc Italian round in the next year was more significant, since MZ works rider Ernst Degner humbled MV's reigning champion Carlo Ubbiali by beating him in a wheel-to-wheel dice at Monza, his home circuit.

The 125cc MZ of 1959 has a deceptively simple air-cooled single cylinder engine, featuring rotary valve induction developed by Kaaden. A slim disc on the crankshaft has a cutaway segment, which uncovers the crankcase inlet port for a precisely timed period as it rotates. This allows mixture to be drawn in under the rising piston from a side-mounted carburettor and gets around restricted intake timings imposed by piston-controlled induction.

Another key element of Kaaden's engine is a third transfer port, added from 1959 to the two normal piston-controlled ports that pass mixture to the combustion chamber as the piston falls. The power-boosting third port is uncovered by a window in the piston skirt. The exhaust port is placed at the rear of the cylinder bore, where thrust on the piston during the power stroke is harnessed to create a superior gas seal, resulting in improved torque. Just as critical in creating usable power is the expansion chamber built into the exhaust pipe, leading into a small diameter tail pipe.

In 1959, the 125 produced a healthy 23PS and the 1961 single reached 25PS, making it the first unsupercharged GP engine to achieve 200PS per litre. But fragility was a problem in long races like the Isle of Man TT.

Degner looked a possible 125cc world champion in 1961, but while leading the series on points, he sensationally defected to the West following the 1962 Swedish Grand Prix and subsequently joined the rival Suzuki team as a development rider.

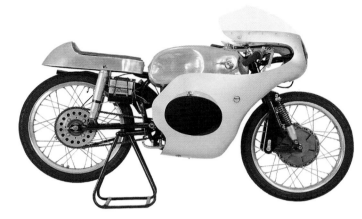

▲ A battery to power the ignition system is carried on one side just below the seat, which like the fuel tank, is fabricated from aluminium sheet. MZ also used magneto ignition.

▼ In 1959 and 1960 this short leading-link front fork was fitted, but handling problems created by escalating power output were eventually overcome by fitting a Norton telescopic fork.

Engine type: Single-cylinder, air-cooled, disc-valve two-stroke
Capacity: 124cc
Bore and stroke: 54mm x 54mm
Compression ratio: 15:1
Fuel system: 27mm Amal carburettor
Power: 23PS @ 10,750rpm
Gearbox: Six-speed
Suspension: Front, telescopic fork. Rear, swingarm with twin shocks
Brakes: Drums front and rear
Dry weight: 68kg
Top speed: 115mph

KAADEN'S CREATION
High-level exhaust runs from a port at the rear of the slightly-inclined cylinder. After Degner moved to Suzuki, MZ concentrated on the 250 and 350cc classes, adopting liquid cooling to ensure reliability and constant power output.

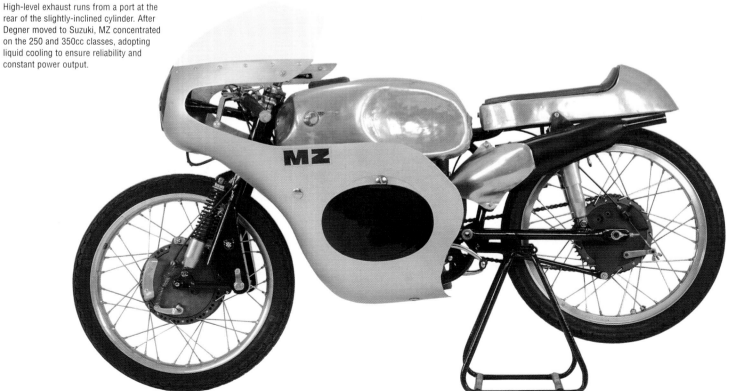

MV AGUSTA

498cc · 1960

MV Agusta utterly dominated 500cc GP racing from 1958 until 1974, winning 17 consecutive individual world championships. To some extent, the factory near Gallarate in Northern Italy had Gilera to thank for its tremendous success. MV's arch rival made winning easier by withdrawing from GP racing after topping the 1957 500cc series, and the Arcore marque had also provided the design basis for MV's all conquering four cylinder machines.

Piero Remor, originator of the 1950s' Gilera in-line four, moved across to MV in 1949 and drew up another 500cc four with shaft final drive. By 1952, MV began to gain rostrum places in GPs and had signed 1949 champion Les Graham who hastened development, notably replacing the shaft with chain drive. Graham's death in a 1953 Senior TT crash set the team back, but with rising British star John Surtees on board, MV developed a 500 good enough to take the title from Gilera in 1956.

For 1958, a 'dolphin' fairing was adopted to suit new FIM rules on streamlining and Surtees won all but one of the 500 GPs to take his second title. He was backed up by team-mate John Hartle and the pair also dominated the 350cc class on smaller fours. With minor improvements, the howling red and silver MVs continued to trounce their less potent rivals after Surtees' departure to car racing at the end of 1960. In the ensuing years Gary Hocking, then Mike Hailwood continued the run of success. It was not until 1967 that the ageing 500 four was finally dropped in the face of Honda opposition, to be replaced by a bigger version of the three cylinder 350 campaigned by Giacomo Agostini since 1965.

Like the Gilera engine, the MV unit has inclined cylinders and drive to the twin overhead camshafts by a train of gears sited between the inner two. Primary gears take drive to the five speed gearbox, above which an ignition magneto is mounted under a bank of four Dell'Orto carburettors.

The twin-loop frame, updated by Surtees in collaboration with MV's brilliant racing team chief Arturo Magni, has a box-section swingarm and a detachable section of tubing to speed up engine removal.

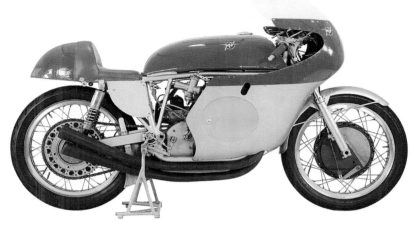

▲ In its 1960 form, the MV Agusta four possessed the power, handling and reliability to make it virtually indomitable in the 500cc GP class for several seasons.

▼ Similar in appearance to the Gilera engine, the MV unit has inclined cylinders and double overhead camshafts disposed at a wide angle. The gearchange pedal is on the right side.

Engine type: In-line four cylinder, air-cooled, double-overhead-camshaft, two-valve four-stroke
Capacity: 498cc
Bore and stroke: 52mm x 58mm
Compression ratio: 10:1
Fuel system: Four 28mm Dell' Orto carbs
Power: 70PS @ 10,500rpm
Gearbox: Five-speed
Suspension: Front, telescopic fork. Rear, swingarm with twin shocks
Brakes: Drums front and rear
Dry weight: 118kg
Top speed: 155mph

DECADE OF DEVELOPMENT
A continuous development programme saw the MV four greatly improved over the original unwieldy shaft drive machines of 1950. The large seat tailpiece and upswept exhaust megaphones are distinctive MV features.

HONDA RC162

250cc · 1961

After making its international racing debut at the Isle of Man TT in 1959, the Honda company launched on the most ambitious multi-class racing programme in the history of GP racing. In the 250cc class, Honda fielded radical high-revving four cylinder engines against the dominant singles and twins of the Italian MV Agusta factory. The Japanese marque's first four to contest GPs was the RC161 of 1960 with inclined cylinders and gear driven double overhead camshafts operating four valves in each combustion chamber. But it was the much improved RC162 of 1961 that blitzed the 250 championship with ten GP victories in the hands of new champion Mike Hailwood, plus Bob McIntyre, Tom Phillis, Kunimitsu Takahashi and Jim Redman. In nine of the eleven rounds, Honda's screaming fours filled the top three places.

The RC162 engine follows traditional Italian four cylinder practice in having an inclined bank of in-line cylinders with cam drive by a train of gears between the inner two. Gears are also used to take drive to the six-speed gearbox. Each Keihin carburettor has an integral floatbowl and sparks are provided by a Kokusan generator. Honda opted for dry sump lubrication of the RC162 engine in the interests of lowering engine weight in the chassis, but this caused problems for team rider Bob McIntyre at the TT. After smashing both the 250 and 350cc lap records at over 99mph he retired when his hot engine ran short of oil and seized. Later Honda reverted to storing oil in the lower crankcase.

The power unit is a stressed frame member, slung below a tubular spine structure and secured, NSU-style, at the rear cambox and in the area of the gearbox. Suspension is by the proven format of a telescopic front fork and rear swingarm with twin shock absorbers. The fairing is fashioned in aluminium, a material soon to be widely replaced by glass fibre mouldings.

Developed to win two more quarter-litre titles in 1962 and 1963, Honda's 250 four was also raced in an enlarged form and a full 350 four was soon developed, enabling Honda to bring an end to MV Agusta's domination of the 350cc class from 1962.

▲ Using four valves per cylinder for efficient breathing, the RC162 was developed to produce 45PS and emitted a deafening howl from its set of four exhaust megaphones.

▼ Powerful braking is achieved by mounting double twin-leading-shoe drum units back-to-back in the front wheel. Each pair of cam operating levers is linked by an adjustable rod.

Engine type: In-line four cylinder, air-cooled, double-overhead-camshaft, four-valve four-stroke
Capacity: 250cc
Bore and stroke: 44mm x 41mm
Compression ratio: 10.5:1
Fuel system: Four Keihin carburettors
Power: 45PS @ 14,000rpm
Gearbox: Six-speed
Suspension: Front, telescopic fork. Rear, swingarm with twin shocks
Brakes: Drums front and rear
Dry weight: 127kg
Top speed: 135mph

QUARTER-LITRE REVOLUTION
The Honda four package includes lightweight build and a slim, efficient fairing as well as engine power. Oil for the dry sump system that was dropped on subsequent fours is carried in a tank under the seat.

CZ

247cc · 1962

Czechoslovakia's CZ (Cseska Zbrojovka) marque arrived on a GP scene dominated by Italian and German machinery in the mid-1950s. It gained some respectable results, most notably the fourth place in the 1957 250cc Isle of Man TT notched by factory rider Frantisek Bartos against a field of highly developed Mondials and MV Agustas.

Founded as an armaments maker, CZ of Stakonice had manufactured two wheelers since the 1930s and from 1948 was part of the nationalised CZ-Jawa combine.

After the 1950s' foray with 125 and 250cc double overhead camshaft singles, CZ withdrew for a few seasons but reappeared with new designs in 1960.

In the 250cc class, CZ campaigned an engine with 'square' bore and stroke measurements of 68 x 68mm and a cylinder inclined at 30 degrees from the vertical. Its camshaft drive was unusual, consisting of a shaft with bevel gears taking drive from the crankshaft to the front, exhaust, camshaft and a second shaft conveying drive to the inlet camshaft.

A further redesign, in which the 250 unit had its bore and stroke dimension altered from 68 x 68mm to an 'over-square' 70 x 64mm and power was boosted to 37PS at 11,000rpm. Factory rider Stanislav Malina began to make some impression on GP results, with a fifth and two sixth places in 1963. He then gained a fortuitous fourth place in the 1964 Lightweight 250cc TT, a race of attrition in which several of the front runners on Japanese factory machines broke down and only eight riders finished. Malina himself was lucky to reach the flag, as spokes had begun to break in his rear wheel.

By the mid-1960s, when Honda and Yamaha were fielding 250s with outputs of 50PS and rising, a single cylinder four-stroke was outpaced. Nevertheless, in 1965 veteran Frantisek Stastny, who more usually rode in GPs under the Jawa banner, managed to score a fourth, two fifths and a sixth place on CZs in 250cc events. And an enlarged 293cc single took Malina to a surprise third place in the 1964 Italian GP, headed by Hondas but in front of Renzo Pasolini's factory Aermacchi single.

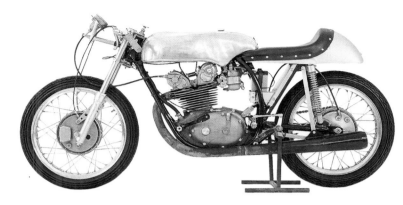

▲ The coil ignition system's battery is carried under the seat and cross-over shafts are used with a left-foot gearchange. The drum brakes have enclosed operating arms.

▼ CZ's unusual camshaft drive with shafts and bevels give the engine a distinctive appearance. Oil supply lines follow the routes of the drive shafts. Lubricant is stored in a wet sump.

Engine type: Single-cylinder, double-overhead-camshaft, two-valve four-stroke
Capacity: 246cc
Bore and stroke: 70mm x 64mm
Compression ratio: n/a
Fuel system: Dell' Orto carburettor
Power: 37PS @ 11,000rpm
Peak torque: n/a
Gearbox: Seven-speed
Suspension: Front, telescopic fork. Rear, swing arm with twin shocks
Brakes: Drums front and rear
Dry weight: 105kg
Top speed: 120mph

REALITY CZECH
Although easily outpaced by Honda, Suzuki and Yamaha fours, the 120mph CZ was competitive against Aermacchi, Benelli and Paton singles.

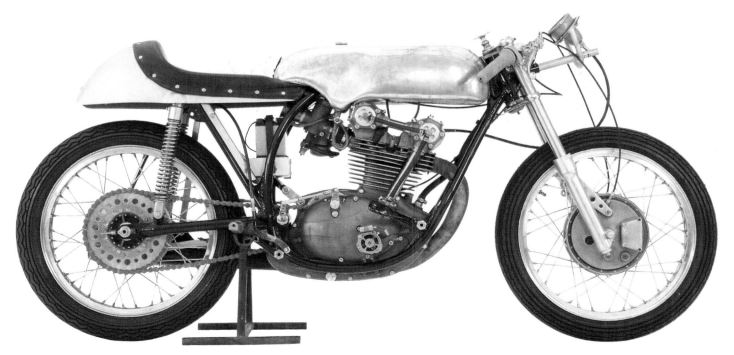

HONDA CR110

50cc · 1962

For 1963 Honda announced its CR series of production racers in a range of cylinder capacities from 50 to 305cc. The most novel of these exclusive machines was the 50cc CR110 Cub Racer, based closely on Honda's factory world championship contender in the 50cc class inaugurated for 1962.

Far superior to anything else available to 50cc class privateers, the CR110 was a four-stroke in a predominatly two-stroke category. Revving to over 14,000rpm, it was not only fast with a top speed approaching 90mph, but rugged and reliable enough for grand prix campaigning.

Its diminutive 49cc single cylinder engine has double overhead camshafts, driven from the crankshaft by a train of gears sited on the right side of the inclined cylinder. Two side-by-side pairs of valves are disposed around a central spark plug, the exhaust items having heads of only 12mm in diameter. With an included angle of 90-degrees between the pairs, they are set in a pent-roof shaped combustion chamber and opened by cam followers sliding in blocks.

The main vertically-split lower casings contain a compact eight-speed gearbox driven by gears via a dry clutch and the sump for the engine's lubrication system. A breather tower behind the cylinder allows the crankcase to vent to the atmosphere while catching oil droplets which can drain back to the sump. Ignition current is supplied from a crankshaft-driven generator.

The light but strong frame is an open-bottomed spine type, relying on the power unit as a chassis stressed member. Drum brakes providing retardation commensurate with the Honda's weight and speed are used on both 18-inch wheels, which are shod with ultra-slim tyres.

Two particular impressions were made by the CR110: its gently tapered exhaust megaphone produced a bellowing sound worthy of a much bigger engine and the relatively wide power band made it easy to ride compared with a two-stroke 50.

In Japan, Honda homologated the CR110 for national racing by marketing a 7PS Cub roadster version. And in 1997 a modern equivalent styled on the CR110 racer, the 5.6PS Dream 50, was produced.

▲ The CR110 offered outstanding performance for its 49cc cylinder capacity, along with sound handling and strong brakes. It was supplied with a fairing and in standard trim had a silver-painted fuel tank.

▼ Mounted at a steep angle, the single Keihin carburettor is of the integral float chamber type Honda also favoured for its factory twin and four cylinder GP machines.

Engine type: Single-cylinder, double-overhead-camshaft, four-valve four-stroke
Capacity: 49cc
Bore and stroke: 40.4mm x 39mm
Compression ratio: 10.3:1
Fuel system: Keihin carburettor
Power: 9.5PS @ 14,000rpm
Gearbox: Eight-speed
Suspension: Front: Telescopic front fork. Rear, swingarm with twin shock absorbers
Brakes: Drums front and rear
Dry weight: 65kg
Top speed: 88mph

LITTLE REVVER
The CR110 embodies typical Honda GP four-stroke technology, using high crankshaft rpm to achieve a maximum of power strokes in a given time. Eight gear ratios are needed to efficiently transfer power to the track.

HONDA RC145
125cc · 1962

Honda's first foray into grand prix racing had been in the 125cc class, with double overhead camshaft twin cylinder machines that were reliable but lacked the speed and handling of the dominant Italian singles.

Honda's earliest RC142 125s of 1959 with shaft-driven camshafts had shown clear NSU influence, no doubt because company chief Soichiro Honda had visited the 1954 TT to research GP technology and the German marque was the most advanced in the lightweight classes at that time. But it was a redesigned RC144 dohc twin, with a central gear train replacing the shaft and bevel camshaft drive that brought Honda its historic first GP win, notched by Tom Phillis at the 1961 Spanish round. Semi-works rider Mike Hailwood clinched that year's 125cc world championship for Honda, while Jim Redman secured the 250cc title with the RC162 four.

In the 1962 125cc series, Honda fielded the further-developed RC145 version of the twin, which enjoyed a spectacular run of success. It won 10 out of 11 grands prix, scooping the first three places at six of them and filling the top five slots at the TT, with diminutive Swiss rider Luigi Taveri emerging as champion.

Revving to 14,000rpm and producing 24PS, the intricate RC162 engine has four tiny valves in each combustion chamber with central plugs sparked by magneto ignition.

As on its 250cc contemporary, the 125's tubular steel open-bottomed frame employs the engine as a stressed member with swingarm and twin shock suspension at the rear. At the front is a simple telescopic fork with internal coil springs and oil damping. Braking is by double single-leading-shoe drums up front and a single twin-leading-shoe unit at the rear. Weighing just over 103kg, the RC145 was the heaviest of Honda's 125s, but its slim, smooth fairing helped it reach 115mph.

A win by Suzuki in the final Argentine round of the 1962 championship heralded a two-stroke challenge to Honda supremacy. Suzuki's latest 25PS disc-valve twin snatched the 1963 title and forced its rival to develop higher-revving four-stroke 125s, first with four and then with five tiny cylinders.

▲ Following Norton practice, Honda's tubular frame has downtubes fixed to the upper part of the steering head and passing between the top tank-support rails.

▼ Rear view shows the Honda's slim aspect, important on a 125cc machine. With no noise restrictions in force, the open exhaust megaphones made a glorious sound.

Engine type: Parallel twin, double-over-head-camshaft, four-valve four-stroke
Capacity: 125cc
Bore and stroke: 44mm x 41mm
Compression ratio: 10.5:1
Fuel system: Four Keihin carburettors
Power: 24PS @ 14,000rpm
Gearbox: Six-speeds
Suspension: Front, telescopic fork. Rear, swingarm, twin shocks
Brakes: Drums front and rear
Dry weight: 103kg
Top speed: 115mph

TITLE-WINNING TWIN
With MV absent from the lightweight classes, Honda faced little opposition to the RC145 twin in the 1962 season, but the company had to develop a four-cylinder 125 to counter Suzuki two-strokes in 1963.

MATCHLESS G50

496cc · 1962

Superseding the Matchless G45 twin, the 500cc G50 single was closely based on the AJS 7R produced within the same Associated Motor Cycles factory. Developed in a collaboration between AMC sales chief Jock West and development engineer Jack Williams, the Matchless single was released for 1959, following race outings by an experimental factory machine during the previous season.

A total of 180 G50s were produced by AMC before it was discontinued after 1962. A far superior machine to the disappointing G45, it was lighter than the rival 500cc Manx production racer made by AMC-owned Norton. Like the AJS 7R, it had the virtue of being simple, making tuning and maintenance easier for private entrants.

Externally similar to the contemporary AJS 7R, the Matchless has a maroon, rather than black, fuel tank. Carburation is by a 38mm Amal GP carburettor and the inlet valve was enlarged from 1960. A well-prepared G50 can produce over 50PS.

It was only after production had ceased that the Matchless began to make an impression in GP events, partly thanks to Essex motorcycle dealer and AMC shareholder Tom Kirby, who entered top class riders on semi-factory singles. In 1963, Alan Shepherd finished runner-up in the 500cc world championship on a Kirby Matchless, behind MV's Mike Hailwood and ahead of 1957 Gilera fours brought out of retirement for that year by Geoff Duke. In 1964, Phil Read rode for Kirby to notch three GP podium places.

Meanwhile, in 1963 the G50 engine took Dick Mann to the national championship in America, where a roadster-framed version had been issued to obtain homologation. And in the following year Selwyn Griffiths notched the first Matchless win in the Senior Manx Grand Prix race on a machine prepared by Welsh tuner Ray Cowles.

Later Peter Williams, son of Jack Williams, put up heroic G50 performances in the TT finishing second four times, the last occasion being in 1974 when he lapped the Mountain Course at a creditable 102.74mph. Entered by Kent haulier Tom Arter, his machine had a special chassis.

▲ The frame is a tubular double cradle type with swingarm and twin shock suspension. The knob on top of the steering head provides adjustment for a friction steering damper.

▼ Sold with a number plate cowl and flyscreen, the G50 was usually raced with a fairing. Flexible gaiters protect the front fork tubes from damage by flying stone chips.

Engine type: Single-cylinder, air cooled, single-overhead-camshaft, two-valve four-stroke
Capacity: 496cc
Bore and stroke: 90mm x 76mm
Compression ratio: 10:1
Fuel system: 38mm Amal GP carburettor
Power: 51PS @ 7,200rpm
Gearbox: Four-speed
Suspension: Front, telescopic fork. Rear, swingarm with twin shocks
Brakes: Drums front and rear
Dry weight: 129kg
Top speed: 138mph (with fairing)

BOY RACER'S BIG BROTHER
The magnesium alloy timing cover, containing the camshaft chain drive and gear drives to the twin oil pumps and ignition magneto, is shaped to enable the exhaust pipe and its megaphone to be well tucked for cornering clearance.

NORTON 30M MANX

499cc · 1962

Despite the technical advances made by factory teams in the 1950s, the single-cylinder Manx Norton continued to be a mainstay of GP grids well into the 1960s.

Norton had a tradition of building batches of production racers, which had originally been directly derived from the company's single-cylinder GP contenders. The Manx name was initiated by a pre-war Manx Grand Prix model and officially adopted when the 350cc 40M and 500cc 30M production racers were made available for the 1947 racing season.

When the works team introduced the revolutionary Featherbed frame in 1950, its benefits were made available to Manx customers for the following season. Even after the factory team was disbanded in the mid-1950s, the production single continued to be refined until finally dropped after 1962.

Built to withstand the rigours of long races, the Manx engine was mostly the work of Joe Craig, Norton's race chief from 1929 to 1955. Sticking doggedly to a simple overhead camshaft single format, he extracted maximum performance from it.

The late-type 500cc Manx has almost 'square' cylinder dimensions of 86 x 85.62mm. The crankshaft is a built-up type with full-circle flywheels and drive for the double overhead camshafts is by a single shaft with bevel and spur gears. The two-valve cylinder head contains a 'squish band' to promote efficient combustion and the Amal GP carburettor is steeply down-draughted. Extensive finning ensures effective air cooling, while ignition is by a chain-driven Lucas 2MTT magneto and a primary chain takes drive to the separate four-speed gearbox.

Giving just over 50PS in standard form, the Norton could approach 140mph on high gearing when fitted with a fairing. It also offered exceptionally stable handling, thanks to the featherbed frame originally designed for Norton by Irish inventor Rex McCandless. One of the final tweaks added for 1962 was a double-sided twin-leading-shoe front brake.

Considered one of motorcycling's all-time classics, the Manx still has a following, evidenced by the continuing production of replicas for historic racing.

▲ The sound handling of the McCandlless featherbed designed frame with swingarm suspension and telescopic front fork allowed skilled riders to use all of the single's power on the track.

▼ Drive to the twin camshafts is by a shaft with bevel gears inside the vertical tube, and spur gears in the cam box. The exhaust pipe is swept back to gain cornering clearance.

Engine type: Single cylinder, air-cooled, double-overhead-camshaft, two-valve four-stroke
Capacity: 499cc
Bore x stroke: 86mm x 85.62mm
Compression ratio: 10.7:1
Fuel system: 38mm Amal GP carburettor
Power: 51PS @ 7,500 rpm
Gearbox: Four-speed
Suspension: Front, telescopic fork. Rear, swingarm with twin shocks
Brakes: Drums front and rear
Dry weight: 142kg
Top speed: 135mph

SINGULAR SUCCESS
For many years a top choice of GP privateers and national racers, the venerated 500cc Manx Norton notched up countless successes but was finally ousted by two-stroke power in the early 1970s.

HONDA CR77

305cc · 1964

The largest and fastest of Honda's CR production racers of the mid-1960s was also the rarest. Used by Honda works riders to race at non-championship events and to back up the team's few 350cc fours at some GPs, the CR77 twin was not distributed in significant numbers like its smaller 50cc CR110 and 125cc CR93 brothers. Similarly, few examples of the 250cc CR72 version fell into private hands.

Although raced in the 350cc class, the CR77 had the unusual 305cc cylinder capacity of the mass-selling CB77 roadster twin also launched in 1963, on which it was closely based. But despite lacking ccs, it proved to be a fast mount. In the 1963 Junior TT, Honda team rider Tommy Robb was timed at 134mph on a slightly downhill part of the course, making his CR77 the second fastest machine in the race behind team mate Jim Redman's four. It was quicker than Gilera and MV fours.

Robb crashed out of the race, but would show the CR77's mettle again at the Italian GP by taking fourth place, later being upgraded when third finisher Remo Venturi was disqualified.

Like other Honda CRs, the 305 has four valves in each combustion chamber. They are operated by double overhead camshafts driven by a train of gears sited between the cylinders, which have separate barrel castings. Following the sohc CB77's layout, the crankpins are disposed at 180 degrees so that one piston is at the bottom of its stroke when the other is at the top and primary gears take drive to the six speed gearbox. Honda tried different frames on its team's CR77s, but the customer version has an open-bottomed type with underslung engine, as on the smaller CRs.

Of the few 305s that did fall into private hands, several were installed in aftermarket frames with the aim of improving the handling. UK rider Dave Simmonds raced a hybrid with a CR77 engine installed in a Norton chassis.

To match the twin's performance, the 19-inch front wheel is fitted with a double-sided twin-leading-shoe drum brake similar to that on full team machines. At speed with a fairing on, only the deeper exhaust note distinguished the twin from a full-factory four.

▲ Long gently-tapered megaphone exhausts emit a deafening bellow. Overall looks are similar to full factory fours of the same period.

▼ Former Honda teamster Ralph Bryans at speed on a privately-owned CR77 at the Assen historic festival in 1998.

Engine type: Parallel twin, double over-head-camshaft, four-valve four-stroke
Capacity: 305cc
Bore and stroke: 60mm x 54mm
Compression ratio: 10.5:1
Fuel system: Two Keihin carburettors
Power: 47PS @ 12,500rpm
Gearbox: Six-speed
Suspension: Front, telescopic fork. Rear, swingarm with twin shock absorbers
Brakes: Drums front and rear
Dry weight: 156kg
Top speed: 130mph

SPEEDY TWIN
Produced when Honda was scaling down its GP involvement, the 305cc CR77 had outstanding performance for a roadster-derived twin, proving competitive against Italian fours.

JAWA

347cc · 1965

Jawa gained very respectable results in 350cc GP racing between 1960 and 1965. During that period the rasping four-stroke twins ridden by Frantisek Stastny and Gustav Havel won three GP victories, seven second and ten third places. They were admirable results given that Jawa's opposition included Honda and MV fours, but despite having a relatively small race shop, Jawa never lacked technical creativity.

The 347cc parallel twins, with slightly inclined cylinders and double overhead camshafts driven by a series of shafts and bevel gears, were developed directly from the less successful 250cc twin.

From 1963, Jawa regularly fielded engines with four valves in each combustion chamber. In these, each camshaft activates four parallel valves via finger-type followers but the format was not adopted permanently because it tended to mar mechanical reliability.

Carburation is by a pair of Amal GP instruments and the two exhaust pipes have gently tapering megaphones with reverse cones. Points-controlled twin-plug coil ignition, as pioneered on the 250cc twin, continued to be used, now with two batteries mounted in an unusual position on either side of the frame downtubes.

Primary drive gears take power to the six speed gearbox via a dry clutch and on the machine shown here a cross-shaft is used to place the gearchange on the right side. Engine oil is stored in a wet sump.

Cycle parts were completely revised in the mid-1960s. A Norton-type double cradle frame with the downtubes and top rails crossing over behind the steering head was dropped in favour of an open-bottomed structure with two main tubes sloping downward from the top of the steering head to the swingarm pivots. The fabricated swingarm incorporates eccentric adjusters at the rear spindle mounts to facilitate tensioning of the drive chain. Twin-leading-shoe drum brakes are fitted front and rear, with a pair of units placed back to back in the front hub.

A significant portion of the slim moulded fuel tank extends down between the upper frame rails to help keep weight distribution low.

▲ The open-bottomed frame used in the mid-1960s was replaced by a double cradle type on the final four stroke twin of 1967, which also sported a larger-diameter drum front brake.

▼ This is the two-valves-per-cylinder 350cc engine. The four-valve type boosted rpm and power output slightly, but at the cost of the reliability needed to amass championship points.

Engine type: Single-cylinder, air-cooled, double-overhead- camshaft, two-valve four-stroke
Capacity: 347cc
Bore and stroke: 59mm x 63.5mm
Compression ratio: 10.5 :1
Fuel system: Two Amal GP carburettors
Power: 46PS @ 11,000rpm
Gearbox: Six-speed
Suspension: Front, telescopic front fork. Rear, swingarm with twin shock absorbers
Brakes: Drums front and rear
Dry weight: 117kg
Top speed: 130mph

TWIN AGAINST FOURS
Jawa's 350cc twins were consistent place-winners behind Honda and MV fours. On a 420cc version, Stastny won the 1966 500cc East German GP after Hailwood's Honda broke down and Giacomo Agostini crashed his MV.

SUZUKI RK65

50cc · 1965

A run of five world championships confirmed Suzuki as the leading marque in the 1960s' heyday of 50cc GP racing. Battling against Derbi, Honda and Kreidler, the Hamamatsu factory developed a series of incredibly compact and, for their capacity, extremely powerful, two-strokes.

The company's European debut was at the 1960 Isle of Man TT, where the team arrived with barely-competitive 125cc air-cooled twins and much to learn about the GP scene.

In mid-1961, MZ development rider Ernst Degner defected to the West and went to Japan to join the Suzuki race team. His input jump-started development, especially in exploiting the latest two-stroke technology used by MZ such as disc valves and tuned expansion chamber exhausts.

Degner won the inaugural 50cc world championship of 1962 for Suzuki and Hugh Anderson took the next two 'tiddler' titles with RM air-cooled singles equipped with eight gear ratios to cope with an inevitably narrow power band.

But by 1965, when Honda's four-stroke twin had the upper hand, Suzuki was responding with the RK65, powered by a liquid-cooled engine with two tiny 25cc cylinders which screamed to 16,500rpm and put 15PS on the road via a 12-speed gearbox.

The RK65 unit has disc valves to time induction of mixture from a 22mm carburettor mounted on each side of the crankcase. A crankshaft-driven Kokusan ignition magneto is sited rearward of the left cylinder and pumps for the liquid-cooling system and positive engine oiling are at the rear of the unit.

To counteract weight added by liquid cooling, the main engine castings are in magnesium alloy and the frame is radical for the period in being made from duralumin alloy tube. The diminutive 100mph Suzuki weighs a mere 60kg. The frame carries the power unit below its tubular structure, with no under-engine rails and rear suspension is by a swingarm and two near-vertical shock absorbers. Both wheels have drum brakes, with two units back-to-back at the front and the 18-inch wheels are shod with very narrow tyres. for minimum rolling resistance.

▲ The expansion chamber exhausts with protective heat shields exit high up to maximise cornering clearance. A sleek fairing helps make efficient use of hard-won power.

▼ Braking for the front wheel is by a double-sided single-leading-shoe drum brake. Judicious use of the brakes is a key part of the specialised technique required for 50cc racing.

Engine type: Parallel twin, liquid-cooled, disc-valve two-stroke
Capacity: 50cc
Bore and stroke: 32.5mm x 30mm
Compression ratio: 8.6:1
Fuel system: Two 18mm Mikuni carburettors
Power: 15PS @ 16,500rpm
Gearbox: Twelve-speed
Suspension: Front, telescopic fork. Rear, swingarm with twin shocks
Brakes: Drums front and rear
Dry weight: 60kg
Top speed: 102mph

TIDDLER TECHNOLOGY
Twin cylinders, liquid cooling for reliability and a 12-speed gearbox to cope with a slender power band were adopted by Suzuki on the RK65 in order to meet the challenge of Honda's 50cc RC115 double overhead camshaft twin.

YAMAHA RD56

250cc · 1965

After a tentative debut on the European scene in 1961, the Japanese Yamaha team headed by Makayasu Nakamura took a year out before launching on what was to be a long and successful GP career with the 250cc RD56. The air-cooled two-stroke twin caused a sensation at the 1963 Isle of Man TT, where it was timed at over 140mph on a fast section of the course and factory rider Fumio Ito finished second to Jim Redman's Honda four in the 250cc Lightweight race after leading in the early stages.

Ito was third in that year's hard-fought 250 championship, further proving the Yamaha's devastating speed with a sizzling record lap of the Spa Francorchamps circuit at 117.82mph in the Belgian round.

In 1964, new signing Phil Read took the improved RD56 to a world title, the first ever to be gained by a two-stroke in the over-125cc GP classes. Read and Yamaha repeated the feat in 1965, even though the engine still proved fragile in long races and arch-rival Honda had a new 250 weapon in the form of its six cylinder four-stroke. To increase both power and reliability, Yamaha developed a liquid-cooled four to replace the RD56, but continued to race the twin while the new machine's various teething troubles were sorted out.

The lower portion of the Yamaha's fairing has a pronounced bulge, so that the moulding can clear the side-mounted carburettors which supply mixture via crankshaft-mounted disc valves. Other key features of the super-fast engine are coated liner-less cylinder bores, three transfer ports per cylinder, squish-band combustion chambers and positive lubrication from a mechanical pump with seven feed lines.

Power for the coil ignition system comes from a generator driven at half engine speed from the gearbox, which contains seven ratios to help riders make the most of a narrow power band. Expansion chamber exhausts precisely shaped to produce optimum power show MZ influence and, reputedly, the Yamaha company's musical instrument expertise was called on to study exhaust resonance during development.

The frame is a double cradle tubular type with a telescopic front fork and rear suspension is by a conventional swingarm with twin shocks.

▲ Elegantly styled as well as being highly competitive, the fully-developed RD56 produced 50PS. Typically for the period, the rear shock absorbers are set almost vertical.

▼ To compensate for the two-stroke engine's lack of engine braking effect, the 1965 RD56 has a powerful double-sided twin-leading-shoe drum front brake.

Engine type: Parallel twin, air-cooled, disc-valve two-stroke
Capacity: 250cc
Bore and stroke: 56mm x 50.7mm
Compression ratio: 10:1
Fuel system: Two 34mm Mikuni carburettors
Power: 50PS @12,000rpm
Gearbox: Seven-speed
Suspension: Front, telescopic fork. Rear, swingarm with twin shocks
Brakes: Drums front and rear
Dry weight: 110kg
Top speed: 145mph

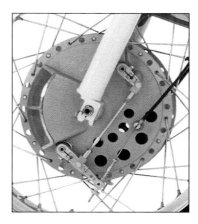

FAST BUT FRAGILE

Yamaha's first successful GP racer, the RD56 won two world championships. The air-cooled twin had a higher top speed than Honda's contemporary 250cc four-stroke fours, but never achieved total reliability.

BULTACO TSS

244cc · 1966

The Spanish Bultaco factory contested grands prix from 1960 until the early 1980s, winning four manufacturer's titles in the 50cc class during the latter years with a machine based on the Italian Piovaticci.

Company founder Francisco Bulto had quit the board of Montesa in 1958 because that marque adopted a no-racing policy. He got his own factory off the ground and developed a 125cc air-cooled single-cylinder two-stroke. It competed in the 1960 TT and was followed by the production TSS125, which rapidly became popular among national-level 125cc racers and private GP entrants.

A bigger TSS196 version followed and for 1965 Bultaco announced its liquid-cooled TSS125 and TSS250 models. As other two-stroke makers had proved, the more constant and comprehensive heat control offered by liquid cooling did not necessarily boost output, but performance was maintained more reliably throughout a race.

The production TSS250 had some build quality shortcomings, but if prepared with care it made a useful simple-to-maintain mount for GP privateers. In 1966 a factory version took Ginger Molloy to Bultaco's first GP win at the Ulster round, after the works Yamahas retired. After fielding a 350 TSS with an air-cooled motocross-type engine, Bultaco concentrated on off-road sport with considerable success.

Sharing a 51.5mm stroke with its 125cc counterpart, the bigger TSS engine has a bore increased from 60 to 72mm, giving an actual capacity of 244cc. The cooling system has no pump, relying on the thermo-siphon effect and there are shallow cooling fins on the iron cylinder and aluminium head castings. Primary drive to the enclosed clutch and five-speed gearbox changed from chain to more reliable gear drive in 1968.

Carburation is by a Spanish-made Amal GP (replaced by a later type of Amal on the example shown here) supplied with fuel into which oil is pre-mixed. One of the best features of the TSS is advanced electronic ignition by the Spanish Femsa company. Although frame materials were not always of the highest quality, Bultaco's road racers were noted for sound handling.

PODIUM POTENTIAL
While not competitive against multi-cylinder rivals, the 250cc Bultaco single notched up several podium finishes in GPs between 1965 and 1968, by which time it was outpaced by Yamaha's TD2 production twin.

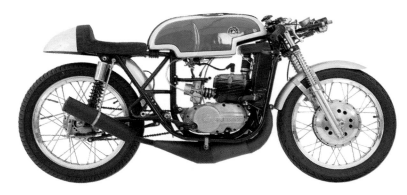

▲ Evolved from earlier air-cooled TSS engines, the liquid-cooled unit has a radiator mounted behind the frame's front downtube. An exhaust silencer has been added to this machine.

▼ A light machine, weighing only 86kg without fuel, the Bultaco handles well and has efficient drum brakes. The power band runs from around 6,000rpm to peak output at 9,200rpm.

Engine type: Single cylinder, liquid-cooled, piston port two-stroke
Capacity: 244cc
Bore and stroke: 56mm x 42mm
Compression ratio: 10.8:1
Fuel system: 30mm Amal carburettor
Power: 36PS @ 10,800rpm
Gearbox: Six-speed
Suspension: Front, telescopic fork. Rear, swingarm with twin shocks
Brakes: Drums front and rear
Dry weight: 86kg
Top speed: 130mph

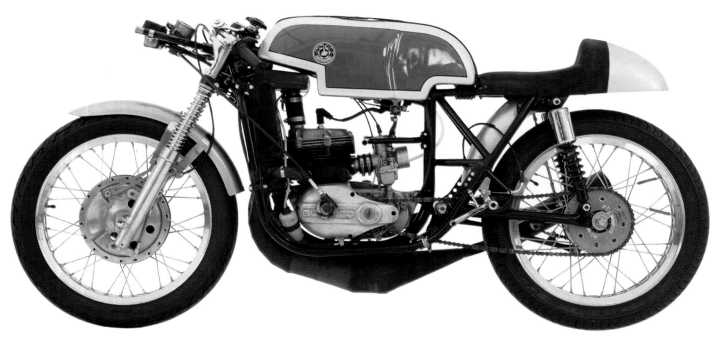

HONDA SIX

250cc · 1966

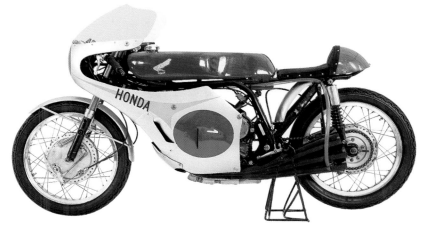

▲ Honda's ultimate 250cc four-stroke is compact, sleek and light despite its mechanical complexity. This privately-owned survivor is used for circuit demos.

Honda's command of the 250cc world championships ended abruptly in 1964, when Yamaha's two-stroke challenge succeeded in wresting the title from the four-stroke fours.

Honda responded with one of the most exotic racers ever built, the 18,000rpm six-cylinder double overhead camshaft RC164. It was unveiled literally, having been hidden under wraps during practice for the 1964 Italian GP. An improved RC165 followed, but it was the RC166 fielded in 1966, when Mike Hailwood had rejoined Honda, which regained Honda the 250cc title.

A marvel of miniaturisation, the six was created by 24 year old engineer Soichiro Irimajiri, who got his high-revving masterpiece from drawing board to test track in a matter of weeks. By 1966 it produced 60PS at a giddy and extremely noisy 18,000rpm.

The compact six-in-line engine's inclined cylinder block is integral with the upper half of a horizontally-split main casing. Gears at the centre of the crankshaft drive the seven-speed gearbox via a jackshaft from which the double overhead camshafts, Kokusan ignition generator and oil pump are driven. Following Honda's established practice, each combustion chamber has two inlet and two exhaust valves disposed around a central spark plug. Induction is by a bank of six 17mm Keihin carburettors with linked lever operation from a single throttle cable. Oil for the wet sump lubrication system is carried in a finned sump under the crankcase. Early overheating toubles were cured by placing oil coolers in the fairing's leading edges.

Handling problems affecting the earlier RC164 chassis were solved by stiffening the tubular frame and fitting Girling rear suspension shock absorbers. The open-bottomed frame uses the power unit as a stressed member, and front suspension is by a conventional telescopic fork. For a complex machine, the RC166 has a low dry weight of 112kg.

The six won ten 250 GPs in 1966 including the Belgian round at Spa Francorchamps, where it lapped at over 122.5mph. In 1967, Hailwood took another 250 title and topped the 350cc class on an enlarged 297cc version.

▼ The view that Honda's opposition usually got of the six in 1966. Arranged to provide cornering clearance, the six individual exhaust megaphones emit a deafening shriek.

Engine type: In-line six cylinder, air-cooled, double-overhead-camshaft, four-valve four-stroke
Capacity: 250cc
Bore and stroke: 39mm x 34.8mm
Compression ratio: 12:1
Fuel system: Four 17mm Keihin carbs
Power: 60PS @ 18,000rpm
Gearbox: Seven-speeds
Suspension: Front, telescopic fork. Rear, swingarm with twin shocks
Brakes: Drums front and rear
Dry weight: 112kg
Top speed: 152mph

SHRIEKING SIX
The high-revving six marked a peak in Honda GP four-stroke development. Withdrawing from the GPs after 1967, the company returned in the 1980s with two-stroke power but reverted to four-strokes for 2002.

KIRBY METISSE G50

500cc · 1966

Late in the 1965 season Tom Kirby, whose Kirby BP race team had enjoyed some success with semi-works AJS 7R and Matchless G50 machines, approached the Rickman company to provide an updated chassis for the single cylinder AMC engines. The Rickman Brothers were a leading maker of specialist motocross frames and marketed kits to accept a variety of engines under the Metisse marque name.

Rickman willingly took on the project and within a few months a slimmer, lower G50-powered road racer was on test. Early in the 1966 season, Kirby's rider Bill Ivy won the 500cc event and set a new lap record at a UK national meeting at Mallory Park, on a Metisse powered by Kirby's works development G50 engine. The team was also supplied with a 350 AJS Metisse.

More machines were built for sale, mostly in kit form to accept existing AMC engines. Rickman also marketed road race chassis to accept other power units, notably Triumph's roadster twins.

Large diameter frame tubing, finished in nickel plate, gives the Kirby Metisse a sturdy look, reinforced by Rickman's own telescopic front fork with 40mm stanchions. In contrast with the dated G50 engine, the hydraulic disc front brake was highly innovative. Based on a design by American racer and tuner Al Gunter, it was developed by Rickman in collaboration with AP Lockheed. The unit features a large conical wheel hub that surrounds the disc rotor. Later Metisse G50s had front and rear discs, with smaller 'cotton reel' hubs. Although highly effective large diameter drum brakes and sophisticated friction materials were available in the 1960s, they suffered from fade, becoming weaker as a race progressed. Heat build up was the principal problem, causing drums to expand away from the shoes and even loosening the wheel spokes.

Following Metisse motocross frame practice, the tubing was designed to carry oil for the dry sump engine, but for enhanced capacity and efficient cooling, a conventional oil tank is fitted under the seat.

A stable, slow-steering machine, the Metisse G50 was to prove less popular than the lighter G50-engined racer from rival frame company Seeley.

▲ A strong structure of mostly straight tubing makes the Metisse chassis very rigid. But some riders found it too stable, giving them no warning of imminent loss of tyre adhesion.

▼ Rickman was the first company to offer a production racing chassis with a disc brake. Lockheed adapted its BMC Mini car caliper to suit motorcycle application.

Engine type: Single-cylinder, air-cooled, single-overhead-camshaft, two-valve four-stroke
Capacity: 496cc
Bore and stroke: 90mm x 78mm
Compression ratio: 11:1
Fuel system: 38mm Amal GP carburettor
Power: 52PS @ 7,200rpm
Gearbox: Four-speed
Suspension: Front, telescopic fork. Rear, swingarm with twin shocks
Brakes: Disc front and drum rear
Dry weight: 127kg
Top speed: 138mph

COMPETITIVE SINGLE
Designed to extend the competitive life of the dated Matchless G50 engine, the Kirby Metisse could not approach an MV four on power but was able take on other single-cylinder machines ridden in the 500cc GP class.

JAWA V4

345cc · 1967

In the early 1960s, Jawa engineers realised the necessity of switching from four-stroke to two-stroke power to be competitive in the 350cc GP class. They produced a series of prototype two-stroke racers from 125 to 350cc, culminating in a liquid-cooled V4.

The 350 Jawa first raced in mid-1967 is of tidy and compact design, despite its complex engine layout. Two crankshafts are mounted one above the other with the lower pair of cylinders set horizontally and facing forward, while the upper pair are inclined upwards at a narrow vee-angle to them.

Four rotary disc inlet valves are located on the crankcase sidewalls, each with its own remote-float Amal carburettor. Ignition was originally by battery and coils with contact breakers, but an electronic system more resilient to high rpm was adopted by 1969.

Gears take drive from the crankshafts to a dry multi-plate clutch and thence to a seven-speed gearbox. The radiator for the simple thermo-siphon cooling system mounts ahead of the upper cylinders, receiving air through an aperture in the fairing.

The power unit is hung in a tubular open-bottomed frame, with main tubes running from the steering head to the rear suspension swingarm pivots and two downtubes running to crankcase mounts. The swingarm is fabricated from oval tube and braced.

Although Jawa obtained 70PS from the four, which produced usable power from 9,000 to 13,500rpm and could reach 160mph, it was plagued by engine seizures. A likely cause was the team's lack of resources relative to Western factories and its inability to obtain the latest and best materials demanded by such a sophisticated engine design.

The V4's only GP victory was scored by Italian rider Silvio Grassetti in the absence of MV Agusta at the 1969 Yugoslavian round. Earlier that year, former Yamaha works rider Bill Ivy was killed when his V4 seized in practice for the East German event. Had this not happened, the team intended him to race a 352cc version in 500cc events. The four had more outings but never realised its promise and the Jawa name faded from the GP scene.

▲ The Jawa four is designed to be as slim as possible with weight kept low in the chassis. Braking is by drums with a double-sided twin-leading-shoe type in the front wheel.

▼ Crankshaft mounted disc valves control the timing of mixture induction from the four side-mounted carburettors. The angle between banks of cylinders is a narrow 18 degrees.

Engine type: V-four, liquid-cooled, disc-valve two-stroke
Capacity: 345cc
Bore and stroke: 48mm x 47.6mm
Compression ratio: 16:1
Fuel system: Four 24mm Amal GP carburettors
Power: 70PS @ 13,000rpm
Gearbox: Seven-speed
Suspension: Front: telescopic fork. Rear, swingarm with twin shocks
Brakes: Drums front and rear
Dry weight: 122kg
Top speed: 160mph

STARVED OF FUNDS
Of ingenious design and producing a competitive 70PS, Jawa's V4 might have achieved much more in 350 and even 500cc GP competition if the Czechoslovakian factory had not been restricted by limited finance.

SUZUKI RK67

50cc · 1967

Defeat by Honda in the 1965 50cc world championship spurred Suzuki to further develop its twin cylinder two-stroke design. It has been said that extracting a gain of 1PS from a 50cc racing engine is as difficult as finding 10PS from a 500, but Suzuki's engineers were becoming expert at squeezing more and more performance from small two-stroke engines. In one mid-1960s project, more than 100 slightly different exhaust expansion chamber forms were tried to produce a mere 2PS gain.

To regain the world title in 1966 Suzuki fielded a subtly revised version of the RK65. Like its predecessor, the RK66 was a liquid-cooled parallel twin with disc-valve induction and rear-facing exhaust ports. But over-winter development saw carburettor size increased from 18mm to 20mm, power output nudged up by 2PS and overall weight reduced by 2kg.

But the most notable feature of the new machine was its transmission. In order to make the most of a slender power band that tended to narrow as rpm and power output were increased, Suzuki produced a gearbox with 14 ratios. Miraculously compact, it was barely more than 200mm wide.

With Honda absent from the 1967 50cc series, Suzuki made sure it utterly dominated the class and the further-developed RK67 won every round. Team orders were used to distribute wins among four factory riders, although a plan for Japanese rider Yoshimi Katayama to win the Isle of Man round went awry when he fluffed his start and then fell off. Former Kreidler teamster Hans-Georg Anscheidt won his second consecutive Suzuki title, with Katayama second and their team-mate Stuart Graham third.

The fourteen-speed RK67 has 22mm carburettors and an output of 17.5PS at 17,300rpm. Otherwise similar to the earlier RKs, it has a water pump to provide forced circulation of the coolant, rather than the less effective thermosyphon system previously relied on.

The power unit is slung from an open-bottomed frame made from lightweight duralumin tubing, also used in swingarm construction. To minimise weight, some chassis parts and fasteners are made of light but strong titanium, later banned by FIM construction rules.

▲ With opposition only from Derbi and Kreidler singles, the fourteen-speed, 110mph Suzuki twin took an easy 1967 50cc title. Cornering clearance on the 18-inch wheels is massive.

▼ Ultimately, a 50cc machine's performance in a race is dependent on rider skill. Carburation is also extremely critical, with settings dictated by even small changes in the weather.

Engine type: Parallel twin, liquid-cooled, disc-valve two-stroke
Capacity: 50cc
Bore and stroke: 54 x 54mm
Compression ratio: 8.5 :1
Fuel system: Two 22mm Mikuni carburettors
Power: 17.5PS @ 17,300rpm
Gearbox: Fourteen-speed
Suspension: Front: telescopic fork. rear: swingarm with twin shock absorbers
Brakes: Drums front and rear
Dry weight: 58kg
Top speed: 110mph

LAST OF THE HYPER-FIFTIES
Suzuki's twin-cylinder power pack includes two 22mm carburettors, a water pump and fourteen gear ratios. Ignition is by a points-less CD system. From 1969, FIM regulations limited machines to one cylinder and six speeds.

LINTO
497cc · 1968

Built to challenge MV Agusta's domination of 500cc GPs, the Linto took its name from its Italian designer Lino Tonti, also associated with Aermacchi, Bianchi and Moto Guzzi. First fielded in 1968 with financial backing from Varese garage proprietor Umberto Premoli, Tonti's twin was capable of 160mph but was plagued by unreliability.

The Linto engine is essentially two 250 Aermacchi single's cylinders side-by-side on a common bottom end, with gear drive to a dry clutch and six-speed gearbox via a countershaft. The pressed-up crankshaft has its big-end journals disposed at 360 degrees, so the two pistons move in unison. Cylinders, heads, pistons and connecting rods are all standard 250cc Aermacchi single components with pushrod operation for two valves in each head. The camshafts are contained in the three-piece main engine casing which also houses the six-speed gearbox and the oil reservoir. Carburation is by vertically-mounted Dell' Ortos and later engines have electronic ignition, a great improvement on the earlier system with contact breaker points. The machine seen here has a Krober electronic rev-counter triggered by the ignition.

The 10,000rpm engine's worst weakness was failure of the countershaft gears, which persisted even after a new type was issued to owners during 1969.

A compact machine with much of its modest weight slung low in the chassis, the Linto handled well after early weaknesses in the trellis-type tubular frame were cured. The front fork is by Ceriani and large diameter drum brakes from both that company and Fontana were used, while the handlebars, control levers and moulded seat are by Menani.

Engine failures and frame breakages plagued works Linto riders Alberto Pagani and Jack Findlay, problems which also frustrated non-factory riders who bought most of the 20-odd Lintos built.

But there were some successes: Pagani won the 1969 Italian GP in MV's absence and Gyula Marzovsky proved that the Linto was the best available privateer's bike by finishing runner-up in the 1969 world 500cc rankings.

▲ Cutaways in the fuel tank allow air to reach the carburettors' vertical intake stacks. Cylinders follow Aermacchi's near-horizontal inclination, keeping weight usefully low.

▼ Frontal view shows overhang of engine unit on the right side. An efficient fairing was used, and a Linto was timed at 162mph in practice for the Irish North West 200 event of 1969.

Engine type: Twin-cylinder, air-cooled, two-valve pushrod four-stroke
Capacity: 497cc
Bore and stroke: 72mm x 61mm
Compression ratio: 10:1
Fuel system: Two Dell' Orto carburettors
Power: 65PS @ 10,000rpm
Gearbox: Six-speed
Suspension: Front, telescopic fork. Rear, swingarm with twin shocks
Brakes: Drums front and rear
Dry weight: 136kg
Top speed: 160mph

ENTERPRISING TWIN
With Giacomo Agostini and his three cylinder MV monopolising the 500cc class in the late 1960s, the fast and loud Linto twin injected much-needed interest in the class but it was let down by fatal mechanical flaws.

SEELEY G50

496cc · 1968

Asuccessful GP sidecar competitor who was third in the 1964 and 1966 world championships, Colin Seeley launched his own racing marque in 1966. He had links with the AMC factory, being based in nearby in South-east London and having raced Matchless outfits in earlier years.

Seeley sponsored solo GP privateer Syd Mizen on a G50 and during 1965 he decided to make the Matchless more competitive by using his own lightweight chassis. The first Seeley racers with Matchless G50 and AJS 7R engines took to the track in 1966 with established star Derek Minter, who achieving immediate success as the team's number one rider.

Buying out AMC's race department when the company collapsed, Seeley was able to put his racers into production and they soon became a favoured choice of leading non-factory riders. Seeley G50s took 13 podium places in 500cc GPs between 1968 and 1971 and gained good results on the Isle of Man TT circuit, where John Blanchard and Alan Barnett lapped at over 100mph on them.

By 1968, Colin Seeley and his senior designer Eddie Robinson had created the MkIII frame. Unlike its predecessors with a double cradle layout, this ultra-light chassis dispensed with downtubes and featured a cross-over arrangement of the top rails and the tubes running from the steering head to the swingarm pivots.

Last of the line was the Seeley G50 MkIV of 1972, equipped with disc brakes and telescopic forks of Seeley's own make. Four-stroke singles were rapidly being rendered uncompetitive by two-stroke engines, but Seeley squeezed more power from the ageing G50 unit. Developments included a long-megaphone exhaust system computer designed Dr Gordon Blair of Queen's University Belfast help boost power output and spread it downwards through the rpm range.

Seeley production ended in 1973, by which time frames and complete machines been built around a variety of engines. Although it was not widely known at the time, some official Suzuki and Kawasaki racers used Seeley frames.

▲ The engine and five-speed gearbox hang from the minimal tubing of the Seeley MkIII frame. As supplied, Seeley rather than Matchless badges were carried on the fuel tank.

▼ New engines were assembled from stocks of parts Seeley had acquired from AMC, or from new components when necessary. The 38mm Amal GP carburettor is standard G50 fitment.

Engine type: single-cylinder, air-cooled, single-overhead-camshaft, four-stroke
Capacity: 496cc
Bore and stroke: 90mm x 78mm
Compression ratio: 11.5:1
Fuel system: Amal GP carburettor
Power: 52PS @ 7,200rpm
Gearbox: Five-speed
Suspension: Front, telescopic fork. Rear, swingarm with twin shocks
Brakes: Drums front and rear
Dry weight: 118kg
Top speed: 140mph (with fairing)

ULTIMATE 500cc SINGLE
Seeley's lightweight chassis and small engine improvements resulted in a single cylinder racer that remained competitive in GPs until 1971. The exhaust system is designed for optimum power and cornering clearance.

YAMAHA RD05A

249cc · 1968

Designed in response to Honda's 250cc six, Yamaha's RD05 stands alongside it as one of the most technically adventurous machines in the history of GP racing. Replacing the RD56 air-cooled twin that propelled Yamaha to glory in 1964 and 1965, the RD05 featured four liquid-cooled cylinders with twin crankshafts.

First raced late in the 1965 season, the four suffered engine reliability and handling problems, the latter causing Phil Read blistered hands on the Isle of Man TT Course in the 1966 Lightweight TT, in which he retired. Also, the sheer complexity of the power unit made the machine bulky, with weight set too high and too far to the rear.

But the RD05 was clearly faster than the Honda six on sheer speed and much of the development work was concentrated on trying to improve its chassis and brakes. It was to be rewarded when Yamaha gained the 250cc world title in 1968 with the much-improved RD05A version of the V4. But with Honda absent from GP racing the most intensive rivalry seemed to be inside the Yamaha team, between eventual champion Read and Bill Ivy.

Ultimately, though, the impending new FIM regulations, which limited 250cc racers to two cylinders and six gears from 1970, spelled the end for exotic machines like the RD05A.

The elaborate V4 engine is essentially a doubled-up version of Yamaha's GP-winning 30PS liquid cooled 125cc twin. The lower crankshaft's forward-facing cylinders are horizontal, while the upper pair tilt slightly forwards. Four side-mounted carburettors supply mixture via disc valves and the upper cylinders' exhaust ports face rearwards, with pipes running to the rear of the machine at high level. A central gear drive transmits power to an eight-speed gearbox via a dry clutch and oil is pumped to 12 points inside the engine. The ultimate RD05A version with electronic ignition produced 70PS at 14,000rpm. A successful 125cc V-four was also raced.

The tubular frame is based on the earlier RD56 type. Chassis development included experiments with a diaphragm steering damper and an adjustable steering stem allowing geometry to be readily altered.

FORMIDABLE FOUR
By adopting a four cylinder engine, Yamaha gained top speed but ran into handling and braking problems. Also, despite the liquid cooling, early fours were unreliable. But the final RD05A version was a superb GP machine.

▲ Several different front brakes were tried on the V-four, which has a top speed of 155mph, and unlike a four-stroke has no engine braking effect when the throttles are closed.

▼ Ignition trigger unit can be seen to the rear of the side-mounted Mikuni carburettors. A radiator for the pumped liquid-cooling system mounts ahead of the upper pair of cylinders.

Engine type: V-four, liquid-cooled, disc-valve two-stroke
Capacity: 249cc
Bore and stroke: 44mm x 40.5mm
Compression ratio: 9:1
Fuel system: Four Mikuni carburettors
Power: 70PS @ 14,000rpm
Gearbox: Eight-speed
Suspension: Front, telescopic front fork. Rear, swingarm with twin shocks
Brakes: Drums front and rear
Dry weight: 115kg
Top speed: 155mph

BENELLI FOUR

414cc · 1969

Although Benelli did not field four-cylinder machinery in GPs until the early 1960s, the factory already had experience of building a complex multi. An amazing supercharged liquid-cooled 250cc Benelli four was completed in 1939, but never raced because of the intervention of World War Two.

Supplanting Benelli's GP single, the second 250cc four made its track debut in 1962. Its potential was shown when Silvio Grassetti defeated works Honda fours in an Italian national meeting, but reliability was poor in the GPs.

Signed for 1964, Tarquinio Provini made a significant contribution to development, winning that year's Spanish GP and the wet Italian GP of 1965.

A 350cc version followed, which by 1966 featured four valves per cylinder, but a crash in that year's TT ended Provini's riding career. His replacement was the fiery Renzo Pasolini, also provided with a bigger four to race in the 500cc class. In 1968, when Honda had withdrawn from the GPs, Pasolini finished runner-up to Giacomo Agostini and his MV in the 350cc world series. In 1969, new signing Kel Carruthers won Benelli the 250 world title with injury-hit 'Paso', who had shown devastating Ago-beating form on the 350 early in the season, finishing third in the series.

The 500cc Benelli four was seen less in GPs, but Pasolini was second to Agostini in Italy in 1968. Mike Hailwood, having a one-off Benelli ride, was fastest in practice but tumbled in the wet race.

The machine seen here is a highly accurate 1990s-built replica of a GP Benelli, created by George Beale in the UK with Italian assistance. It is a large-bore version of the 1969 350, with a cylinder capacity of 414cc.

Unlike Honda and MV fours, the 1960s' Benelli engine has upright cylinders. Drive to the double overhead camshafts is by a central train of gears and primary drive to the gearbox, which on this machine has has seven ratios, is also by gears. Each cylinder has four valves with a central plug and ignition is supplied by a marine magneto.

Benelli built updated 350 and 500cc fours with inclined cylinders, and Finnish rider Jarno Saarinen won an Italian non-championship race on them in 1971. But then the inconsistent Benelli factory faded from the GP scene.

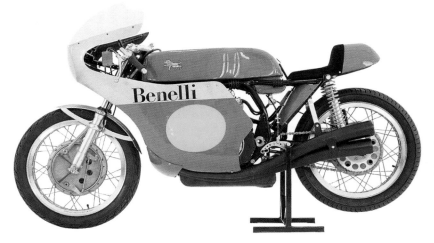

▲ The engine's oil sump protrudes into the airstream through the bottom of the fairing. Four elegantly curved exhaust megaphones emit an awesome howl at full throttle.

▼ The engine breathers are routed to an oil collector box fixed to the rear mudguard moulding, with a single outlet tube venting into the upper right-side exhaust pipe.

Engine: In-line four cylinder, air-cooled, double-overhead-camshaft, four-valve four-stroke
Capacity: 414cc
Bore and stroke: 56mm x 42mm
Compression ratio: 11.5:1
Fuel system: Four 30mm Dell 'Orto carbs
Power: 70PS @ 11,000rpm
Gearbox: Seven-speed
Suspension: Front, telescopic fork. Rear, swingarm with twin shocks
Brakes: Drums front and rear
Dry weight: 150kg
Top speed: 155mph

HEAVYWEIGHT CONTENDER
Lacking the depth of development of its rivals, the Benelli was heavy at 150kg. Front fork and brakes are by Ceriani, with a double-sided twin-leading-shoe drum on the front wheel.

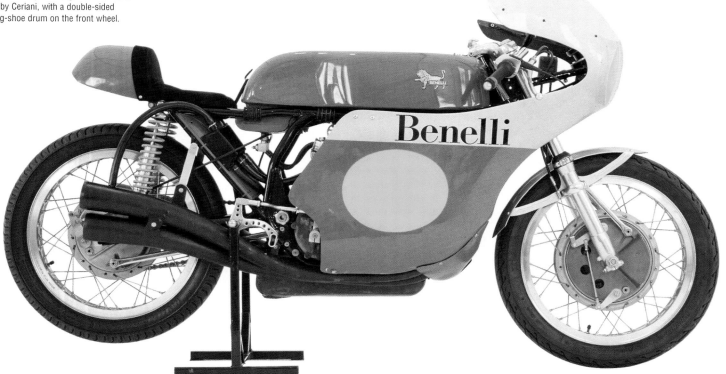

PATON

480cc · 1969

The Paton marque has made an impression on the GP scene out of all proportion to its tiny size and tight financing.

After Mondial withdrew from racing in 1957, the team's chief mechanic Giuseppe Pattoni joined engineer Lino Tonti in a small Milanese workshop to build their own racing machines. Forming the Paton name from the first letters of Pattoni and Tonti, their first products were dohc conversions for production Mondials. Tonti moved on in 1959 and Pattoni persevered, often on a part-time basis. His first Paton twin was a 250 and its reliability saw it take Alberto Pagani to a surprise third place in the 1964 Lightweight TT. A 350cc twin followed, eventually acquired by Liverpool-based businessman Bill Hannah who backed Pattoni to build a batch of 500cc twins. While not in the same league as the works MV Agusta, they were faster than privateers' ageing British singles and scored good results. Angelo Bergamonti defeated Giacomo Agostini and his MV in the 1967 Italian Senior championship on a works Paton and Billie Nelson was fourth in the 1969 500cc world rankings.

Although Pattoni was always short of funding, he used his inventive mind to make machines as competitive as possible. The 500 engine is a sturdy high-revving 180-degree dohc parallel twin. Internal gear drives are used extensively. A toothed sleeve linking the two halves of the crankshaft turns a countershaft from where drive is taken to the camshaft gear train, the oil pump and coil ignition contact breakers, as well as to the six-speed gearbox. The engine's oil sump is bolted on, differing sizes being used according to race conditions. A final version of the dohc 500cc twin had four-valve combustion chambers.

Built with small diameter tubing, Paton's double cradle swingarm frames are characterised by a very short wheelbase, making for enhanced cornering agility. A Ceriani front fork is used and braking is by Fontana drums, the most powerful available at the time, with a gigantic 250mm double-sided twin-leading-shoe type up front.

Pattoni's son Roberto currently runs a modern GP team, fielding a 500cc two-stroke bearing the Paton name.

▲ Pattoni's 500cc engine has double overhead camshafts driven by a central gear train, via a countershaft. An uprated version with four valves per cylinder raced from 1970 to 1974.

▼ One of the few surviving 500cc Patons in action at a historic racing festival in the 1990s. Its 250mm Fontana double sided twin-leading-shoe front drum gives powerful braking.

Engine type: Parallel twin, air-cooled, double-overhead-camshaft, two-valve four-stroke
Capacity: 480cc
Bore and stroke: 73mm x 56mm
Compression ratio: 11:1
Fuel system: Two 40mm Dell' Orto carburettors
Power: 64PS @ 10,400
Suspension: Front, telescopic fork. Rear, swingarm with twin shocks
Brakes: Drums front and rear
Dry weight: 140kg
Top speed: 150mph

SHORT AND SWEET
With 150mph capability and agile handling, Pattoni's ingenious creation added spice to the 500cc GP class in the late 1960s, when there were all too few machines in the same league as the three-cylinder MV Agusta.

DERBI

50cc · 1970

The Spanish Derbi two-stroke factory made its mark in 50cc racing from the inaugural year of the 'tiddler' class in the FIM series. At the 1962 Spanish GP, the first world championship meeting to include a 50cc race, Derbi's factory rider Jose Busquets delighted the Barcelona crowd by taking a close second place behind Hans-Georg Anscheidt's Kreidler and coming home ahead of the works Hondas.

In the years that followed, it became increasingly difficult for the small Derbi marque to compete with Honda and Suzuki, whose rivalry resulted in increasingly sophisticated 50s. But in the absence of other works teams, Australian Barry Smith scored an easy win for Derbi in the 1968 TT and was third in that year's world rankings. Then, new FIM rules restricting the 50s to single cylinder engines and six-speed gearboxes from 1969 gave Derbi its chance. The company finally achieved GP glory by taking hard-fought world championships in 1969, 1970 and 1972 with factory rider Angel Nieto aboard. He was the first Spanish rider to win a world championship.

Seeing GP success as a powerful marketing tool for its lightweight road motorcycles, Derbi had persisted with steady development, moving from its air-cooled 12.5PS contender of 1962 to the low-slung 120mph liquid-cooled 14,000rpm screamer of the early 1970s. Improvements in output were due to painstaking work and the availability of better materials.

Designed to keep frontal area to a minimum and reduce air drag, the diminutive Derbi has a near-horizontal cylinder with the carburettor and disc valve situated on the left side of the crankcase. The tubular frame has twin shock rear suspension, front suspension by telescopic fork and braking by drums, with a double sided twin-leading-shoe unit at the front.

The Derbi factory withdrew from GP racing after 1972 but released a Nieto replica very similar in appearance to the works type but with air-cooling and not in the same speed league, sadly not as fast as the works type. The factory returned to contest the 80cc class inaugurated in the 1980s and in recent 125cc GPs, the L&M Derbi team has been prominent, its riders including Pablo Nieto, one of Angel Nieto's three racing sons.

SPANISH FLIER
Attention to development enabled Derbi to step up to the 50cc winner's podium when Suzuki withdrew from the world championship after 1967.

▲ Compact and low-slung, the Derbi was tailored to suit riders of small stature, as 50cc specialists almost inevitably were. Front fork is by Ceriani and drum brakes by Fontana.

▼ Frontal view shows the Derbi's aerodynamic shape, developed with the aid of a wind tunnel at a Spanish military establishment. Sound handling was also a key to success.

Engine type: Single-cylinder, liquid-cooled, disc-valve two-stroke
Capacity: 50cc
Bore and stroke: 40mm x 39.5mm
Compression ratio: n/a
Fuel system: Dell' Orto carburettor
Power: 15.5PS @ 14,500rpm
Gearbox: Six-speed
Suspension: Front, telescopic fork. Rear, swingarm with twin shock absorbers
Brakes: Drums front and rear
Dry weight: 65kg
Top speed: 120mph

HARLEY-DAVIDSON RR250

246cc · 1972

Already famous for its four-stroke singles, the Italian Aermacchi factory realised by the early 1970s that two-stroke power was its only hope of remaining competitive. The Italian plant, part-owned by America's Harley-Davidson since 1960, had developed a single cylinder 125cc two-stroke and this was used as a basis for a 250cc twin first fielded in 1971.

Redesigned for the following season, the RR250 in Harley-Davidson's black and orange racing colours took works rider Renzo Pasolini to three Grand Prix wins over Yamahas in Italy, Yugoslavia and Spain. He also won the Italian national championship, while French rider Michel Rougerie rode one to victory in his country's 250cc national series. A 350 version was fielded in 1972, as well, reliably taking Pasolini to third place in the world championship.

Further development saw the air-cooled 250 and 350cc engines replaced by liquid-cooled units, but the H-D team suffered a set-back when Pasolini was killed in a multiple accident at the 1973 Italian GP, in which rising Yamaha star Jarno Saarinen also lost his life. But with Walter Villa as team number one, four titles were notched in both the 250 and 350cc classes from 1974 to 1976.

Conceived by Aermacchi design chief William Soncini, the 1972 air-cooled RR250 produced over 50PS, compared with the earlier 250cc four-stroke's 36PS. Of simple modular construction, with separate cylinder and head castings, a compact crankcase and separate six-speed gearbox, the parallel twin relies on piston port induction without reed valves, while its pistons run in plated cylinder bores. The engine is designed for ease of maintenance, repair and part substitution, useful on a high performance two-stroke in the heat of a GP meeting.

The frame is tubular with rear suspension by swing arm and twin shock absorbers. The front fork is a Ceriani component and the same company provided this machine's drum brakes, an effective double-sided 230mm unit being fitted at the front. Later H-D two-stroke racers sported an unusual Campagnolo hub brake with a conical friction surface and hydraulic operation.

▲ H-D's second generation air-cooled 250cc two-stroke won three GPs in 1972, but liquid cooling had to be introduced to remain competitive in subsequent seasons.

▼ Drum brakes made by Ceriani were used both by GP works teams and private entrants. This unit has a pair of twin-leading-shoes on each side, with adjustable external linkages.

Engine type: Parallel twin, air-cooled, piston port, two-stroke
Capacity: 246cc
Bore and stroke: 56mm x 50mm
Compression ratio: 12:1
Fuel system: Two 30mm Mikuni carburettors
Power: 50PS @ 11,400rpm
Gearbox: Six-speed
Suspension: Front, telescopic fork. Rear, swingarm with twin shocks
Brakes: Drums front and rear
Dry weight: 112kg
Top speed: 145mph

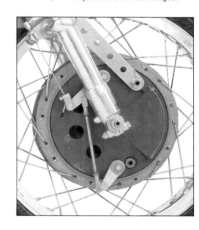

ITALIAN CHALLENGER
Simple enough to be rebuilt with hand tools in the race paddock, the 50PS piston port two-stroke engine and its six-speed gearbox are mounted in a tubular frame that was retained for the 1973 liquid-cooled version.

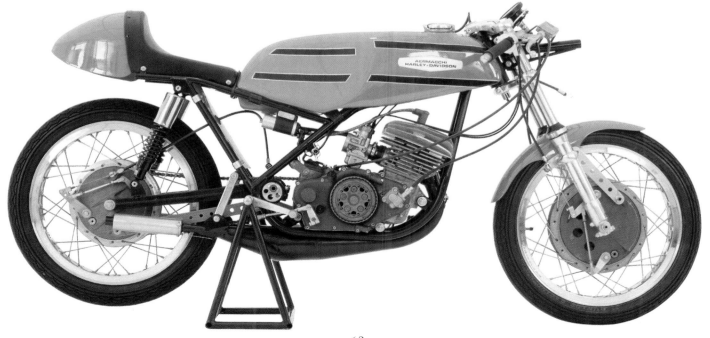

MAICO RS125

124cc · 1974

The long-established German Maico company made a dramatic entry to GP racing in 1969, when its new RS125 single finished second in the 125cc Spanish GP, ridden by Kent Andersson. And continuing successes saw the Swedish rider finish fourth in the world rankings on the works version of Maico's roadster-based two-stroke production racer.

When Andersson moved on to Yamaha, he was replaced by another Swede, Borje Jansson, whose stirring performances hoisted Maico to third place in the 1970 championships behind Dieter Braun's Suzuki and Angel Nieto's Derbi, gaining five podium places. Reigning champion Braun joined Maico for the next season, but it was Jansson who brought the factory its first GP victory at the 1972 East German event, shortly followed by a win in Czechoslovakia and consolidated by another at the 1973 Swedish GP. Maico's fourth GP win was scored by Fritz Ritmaier at the 1974 West German event, where the host country's 125s dominated the race by filling five of the first six places.

The basic RS125 engine featuring an inclined air-cooled cylinder and disc valve induction from a side-mounted carburettor was the work of Maico engineer Gunther Schier. He used existing road and motocross units as a basis for what became an excellent production racer capable of nearly 120mph and a winner in countless events below GP level.

The factory team, and some independent tuners, converted to liquid cooling to maintain boosted power output throughout long races.

From 1971, works machines sported a 'lowboy' frame with its top rails turning down to meet the seat support tubes and a rearward portion of the fuel tank projecting downwards to keep weight low. An Italian Ceriani front fork was fitted, with a double-sided twin-leading-shoe drum brake of the same make for the front wheel.

Maico's own liquid-cooled engine has a forward-facing exhaust port with the radiator mounted just above it and coolant is pumped by an impeller behind the crankshaft. All RS125s have six speed gearboxes, in line with the maximum number of ratios imposed by the FIM from 1969.

▲ Lowboy frame helps achieve better weight distribution than the production RS125. Factory machines also sport a Ceriani drum front brake and beefed-up rear suspension swingarm.

▼ A Bing carburettor with an integral floatbowl supplies mixture to the crankcase via a rotating disc valve. The flywheel ignition magneto is at the other end of the crankshaft.

Engine type: Single-cylinder, liquid-cooled, disc-valve two-stroke
Capacity: 124cc
Bore and stroke: 54 x 54mm
Compression ratio: 15:1
Fuel system: 34mm Bing carburettor
Power: 28PS @ 11,500rpm
Gearbox: Six-speed
Suspension: Front, telescopic fork. Rear, swingarm with twin shocks
Brakes: Drums front and rear
Dry weight: 70kg
Top speed: 120mph

SOLID PERFORMER
A simple but sturdy machine, Maico's RS125 single held its own against Derbi and Yamaha twins, notching 4 wins and 29 podium places in 125cc GPs between 1969 and 1974.

MV 350

350cc · 1974

After adopting an in-line three-cylinder layout for its 350 and 500cc GP machines in the mid-1960s, MV Agusta developed a new generation of fours to defend its proud GP record into the next decade.

Honda took over MV's 350cc mantle in the 1960s, but after the Japanese factory's withdrawal Giacomo Agostini rode his Italian triple to four world championships from 1968 to 1971. But a new 350cc threat loomed in the form of Yamaha's production-based air-cooled twin, especially in the hands of talented young Finnish rider Jarno Saarinen.

Resolutely committed to four-stroke power, MV prototyped a 350 six, but it was dropped when the FIM announced coming limits on the number of cylinders for GP classes. A high-revving four-valve four was developed instead and rushed into action after Saarinen won 1972's first two 350cc GPs for Yamaha. Agostini notched six rounds on the four and retained the title, proving the enduring technical prowess of the MV team led by Arturo Magni.

'Ago' took another 350 title in 1973, but Yamaha was piling on pressure both in that class and now in the 500cc GPs, where an enlarged MV four was provided for MV's other teamster Phil Read. In 1974, Agostini made a sensational move to Yamaha and became the first rider to win a 350 world title on a two-stroke. MV had abandoned the class early in the season, but Read gained the factory its final 500cc crown on the bigger four.

Like the older fours, the 1970s version has inclined in-line cylinders, with drive to the double overhead camshafts by a central gear train. But the compact later unit has a much narrower valve angle to achieve an optimum combustion chamber form. It breathes through four Dell' Orto carburettors, varied in size from 28 to 32mm according to circuit conditions. MV's cassette-type six speed gearbox, allowing internal ratios to be altered to suit particular circuits and conditions, has since become a normal feature on GP racers.

Having proved his previous titles were not merely due to MV's superior machinery, Agostini returned to the Italian team for 1976. He won that year's 1976 350cc Dutch TT on MV's further-developed 77PS four, the last four-stroke to win a GP race under pre-2002 formulae.

▲ Although state-of-the art for a four-stroke of the period, the 350 of 1972-1974 retained classic MV looks. The under-engine oil sump projects downwards between the exhaust pipes.

▼ MV Agusta was the first leading GP team to adopt disc brakes and solid cast wheels. Two hydraulically-operated Lockheed calipers and cast iron disc rotors are fitted at the front.

Engine type: In-line four-cylinder, double-overhead-camshaft, four-valve four-stroke
Capacity: 350cc
Bore and stroke: 53mm x 39.5mm
Compression ratio: 12:1
Fuel system: Four Dell' Orto carburettor
Power: 70PS @ 16,000rpm
Gearbox: Six-speed
Suspension: Front, telescopic fork. Rear, swing arm with twin shocks
Brakes: Discs front and rear
Dry weight: 122kg
Top speed: 160mph

FOUR-STROKE FINALE
A high-revving short-stroke engine kept two-strokes at bay, but high output relied on a noisy open-megaphone exhaust system. Spectators loved the sound, but a 1976 FIM noise limit spelled the end for MV's four-strokes.

SUZUKI XR14

498cc · 1975

Suzuki's first 500cc GP victory was in the 1975 Dutch GP, when Barry Sheene beat Giacomo Agostini and his Yamaha aboard the four-cylinder XR14/RG500. Prior to that, Suzuki's world championship success had been confined to the 50cc and 125cc classes, but Sheene's victory was the prelude to a Suzuki blitz of the half-litre category.

The XR14 was first wheeled out for 1974, when it proved fast and gained promising results, but handling could be unpredictable and it was dangerously liable to seizure both in the engine and the six-speed gearbox. However, with significant chassis revisions and a winter of further development, the Suzuki returned to the 1975 GPs as a truly competitive machine.

Like Suzuki's GP 250s of the 1960s, the XR14 designed by Makoto Hase is a liquid-cooled two-stroke with disc valve induction and 'square four' cylinder arrangement. Four independent crankshafts are geared to a large primary drive pinion taking power to a six-speed gearbox. Round-slide carburettors with lightweight magnesium alloy bodies mount directly to the crankcase walls, where crank-mounted disc valves give precise induction timing for maximum output. Five piston ports in each bore control transfer and exhaust functions, the upper cylinders having rearward facing exhaust pipes that exit alongside the seat fairing. Ignition is by a magneto placed at the left end of the primary gear countershaft.

Suzuki had to work hard to develop chassis components that could match its 500's power output, up to 100PS in 1975. An early open-bottomed tubular frame was replaced with a full cradle type during 1974, and tilting the rear shock absorbers forward at an acute angle improved the handling. Cast magnesium alloy wheels were also adopted by late 1974 and the performance of the triple-disc braking system was improved.

Suzuki stood back from the GPs from 1976 but supplied updated RG500-series machines to Europe-based teams. Sheene won two consecutive 500cc titles in 1976 and 1977 for Suzuki GB, while Marco Lucchinelli and Franco Uncini were to take two more 500cc titles with the Italian Gallina organisation.

▲ Cast wheels and steeply-angled rear shock absorbers were among changes made during the 1974 development season. The screeching XR14 was Suzuki's last unsilenced GP machine.

▼ Barry Sheene re-united with his 1975 Suzuki at the Assen Centennial TT festival in 1998. The pairing scored Suzuki's first 500cc GP victory at the Dutch circuit in 1975.

Engine type: Square four, liquid-cooled, disc-valve two-stroke
Capacity: 498cc
Bore and stroke: 56mm x 50.5mm
Compression ratio: 8:1
Fuel system: Four 34mm Mikuni carburettors
Power: 100PS @ 11,200rpm
Gearbox: Six-speed
Suspension: Front, telescopic fork. Rear, swingarm with twin shocks
Brakes: Discs front and rear
Dry weight: 135kg
Top speed: 175mph

FIRST OF A WINNING LINE
The innovative four-crankshaft XR14/RG500 thrust the company to the fore in 500cc GP racing and was the basis of the successful RG500 production racer.

MOTOBECANE

124cc · 1980

Although it was up against stiff competition from the Italian MBA and Minarelli marques, the 1980 works Motobecane was highly competitive, taking three wins and three second places in that 125cc GP season. Indeed, if team rider Guy Bertin hadn't crashed in the British and Spanish rounds, he would probably have won the world championship.

The French factory was relatively new to the GP scene, although Motobecane products were a familiar sight on the country's roads. An air-cooled 125cc two-stroke production racer had been developed in the early 1970s, followed by a factory water-cooled twin aimed at GP level. In its first form this proved uncompetitive, but a new 44PS version created by chief designer Jean Bidalot gained promising results in 1979 both for Thierry Espie and Bertin, who won the last two GPs of the season. But after his superb Pernod-sponsored 1980 showing, Bertin switched to the Sanvenero team and key engineer Bidalot departed to develop a 250 GP bike raced under the Pernod name. After Jacques Bolle took fifth place in the world 125 rankings on a Motobecane in 1981, the marque which had shown such promise disappeared as a force in GP racing.

A parallel twin with its cylinders set almost horizontally to keep weight low, the 125cc GP engine uses disc valve induction, breathing through 29mm Mikuni carburettors located on each side of the crankcase. Four ports in each cylinder transfer mixture to the combustion chamber and the single exhaust ports exit into expansion chamber pipes. Gears drive a six-speed gearbox contained in a housing machined from a billet of aluminium, via a dry clutch. The engine cooling system's radiator is placed in the nose of the fairing.

The light and low-slung frame tubular frame has straight top tubes rigidly linking between the steering head and swingarm pivot, where eccentric mountings allow the pivot to be moved to adjust drive chain tension. A pair of Marzocchi shocks absorbers control the rear suspension's box-section swingarm while a telescopic fork of the same make is used up front. Braking for the five-spoke cast magnesium wheels is by three hydraulic discs.

▲ Power output equivalent to over 350PS per litre and superb handling made the Motobecane an excellent GP prospect. From 1987, GP 125s were restricted to single cylinders.

▼ The liquid-cooling system's radiator is placed in the fairing nose and doubles up as the front number plate. This helps keep frontal area to a minimum, vital on small capacity racers.

Engine type: Twin-cylinder, liquid-cooled, disc-valve two-stroke
Capacity: 124cc
Bore and stroke: 44mm x 41mm
Compression ratio: 8.8:1
Fuel system: Two Gurtner carburettors
Power: 44PS @ 14,000rpm
Gearbox: Six-speed
Suspension: Front, telescopic fork. Rear, swingarm with twin shocks
Brakes: Discs front and rear
Dry weight: 80kg
Top speed: 130mph

FRENCH LESSON
Raced during a period when minor European makes monopolised the 125cc GP class, Motobecane's 44PS contender came close to gaining the first world championship for a French manufacturer.

SUZUKI RG

495cc · 1980

As soon as its four cylinder 500cc RG500/XR14 had been developed to GP-winning level in 1975, Suzuki put a similar machine into limited production for the use of teams and privateer riders. The first competitive 500cc production racer since Matchless G50 and Manx Norton days, Suzuki's RG500 two-stroke incorporated 20 years of technical progress and was closer in performance to factory GP machinery of its period.

Closely modelled on the factory RG500, the customer version followed it through a series of engine and chassis updates from the very few early MkI versions supplied in 1975, up to the much-modified MkIX of the early 1980s.

As on the 500cc works racers, the liquid-cooled cylinders are arranged in square formation with separate crankshafts driving a main primary gear below them which transmits power to a six-speed gearbox via a dry multi-plate clutch. Two carburettors are mounted on each side of the engine, each feeding its cylinder's crankcase directly via a disc valve. On factory racers, the layout was changed in 1978, placing the rear pair of cylinders higher than the front two. This made rapid changes of internal gearbox ratios possible, as well making the power unit, and thus the whole machine more compact. Production RG500s followed suit from 1981.

Earlier versions had swingarm rear suspension with twin shock absorbers, replaced in 1981 by Suzuki's 'Full Floater' monoshock system introduced on XR34 works machines in the previous season. Front suspension was updated, passing on factory experience with a hydraulic anti-dive system that restricts the rate of damping to inhibit fork plunge during heavy application of the twin disc front brake. The final production version had an aluminium frame.

With its relatively broad power band, and useful 180mph top speed, the RG500 was a mainstay of 500cc GP grids and after complete machines ceased to be available, some bare engines were supplied for three seasons.

The machine seen here is finished in the colours of Team Gallina, Italy's official Suzuki squad sponsored by Nava helmet company. Team rider Marco Lucchinelli won the 1981 500cc world title on a factory RG500/XR35.

▲ The rear cylinders' exhaust pipes are arranged to emerge through each side of the extensive seat fairing. The aluminium swingarm is well braced and cast wheels are fitted.

▼ Marco Lucchinelli back on a Suzuki RG500 at the 1998 Assen Centennial. In 1981, the Suzuki's superior handling helped him defeat Yamaha's reigning champion Kenny Roberts.

Engine type: Square four, liquid-cooled, disc-valve two-stroke
Capacity: 495cc
Bore and stroke: 54mm x 54mm
Compression ratio: 9:1
Fuel system: Four Mikuni carburettors
Power: 110PS @ 11,000rpm
Gearbox: Six-speed
Suspension: Front, telescopic fork. Rear, swingarm with twin shocks
Brakes: Discs front and rear
Dry weight: 136kg
Top speed: 180mph

TOOL FOR THE JOB
A godsend for non-factory riders seeking glory in the 500cc class, the Suzuki RG500 offered speed, sound handling and a high degree of tractability for a disc valve two-stroke.

KAWASAKI KR500

495cc · 1981

Campaigned from 1980 to 1982, Kawasaki's KR500 grand prix contender was a four-cylinder version of the 250 and 350cc two-stroke twins which had convincingly won their class world championships in 1978 and 1979, ridden by Kork Ballington. But unlike them, the KR500 had a monocoque chassis fabricated in sheet metal and instead of a 'tandem' twin layout the 500 unit has four cylinders in square formation.

Roughly similar to Suzuki's RG500, the Kawasaki differs in having its cylinders inclined forwards. Disc valves on the four crankshafts control induction timing, with mixture supplied by four magnesium-bodied Mikuni round-slide carburettors. The upper pair of cylinders have rearward-facing exhaust ports and their expansion chamber pipes exit on either side of the tail fairing. Ignition is by a magneto on the leftward end of the primary drive countershaft below the crankcases. The lower engine cases can be readily removed for changing the six internal gearbox ratios to suit different circuits.

Using a construction method pioneered in GP racing by the Spanish Ossa company in the late 1960s, the KR500 frame is welded-up from sections of aluminium sheet. The 1982 version has a box section spine inside a separate removable fuel tank. The front fork features a mechanical anti-dive system to maintain suspension travel under hard braking and adjustable yokes for changes to steering geometry. Unsprung weight is reduced by aluminium front brake discs with alloy billet calipers. Rear suspension is by Kawasaki's Uni-Trak system with a triangulated swingarm connected to the single shock via a rocker-link.

Although the KR500 eventually found competitive top speed, it struggled for places against Suzuki's square four and Yamaha's in-line four, both with more extensive development behind them. A long wheelbase helped the KR500's straight-line stability but hampered cornering agility. Despite dubious handling, Ballington managed two third places in 1981 GPs, in the Dutch and Finnish rounds, to place him ninth in the world championship rankings. With lower placings but more consistency, he got the same result with the revised machine in 1982.

▲ Ingenious chassis technology includes the front fork's mechanical anti-dive system and billet-type brake calipers. The three-spoked wheels are cast in magnesium alloy.

▼ Light but extremely rigid, the welded aluminium monocoque chassis incorporates a conventionally located 32-litre fuel tank. Screwed-on sideplates carry the footrests.

Engine type: Four-cylinder, liquid-cooled, disc-valve two-stroke
Capacity: 495cc
Bore and stroke: 54mm x 54mm
Compression ratio: n/a
Fuel system: Four 34mm Mikuni carburettors
Power: 120PS @ 11,000rpm
Gearbox: Six speeds
Suspension: Front, telescopic front fork. Rear, Uni Trak monoshock
Brakes: Discs front and rear
Dry weight: 138kg
Top speed: 190mph

HIGH-TECH LOSER
A host of interesting features and an output of 120PS were not enough to win 500cc GP glory for Kawasaki. The company had won eight 250 and 350cc manufacturers's titles when it ceased GP racing after 1982.

YAMAHA OW48R

498cc · 1981

After becoming the first factory to win a 500cc world championship with a two-stroke in 1975, Yamaha was locked into a protracted battle with Suzuki for class supremacy. Barry Sheene gained Suzuki two titles in 1976 and 1977, but Yamaha's talented American rider Kenny Roberts came back with a hat-trick of 500cc championships from 1978 to 1980.

To clinch the third title, Yamaha wheeled out its OW48. Like earlier YZR500s, it had a liquid-cooled in-line four cylinder engine with simple piston port induction: reed valves were dropped after 1975. And it incorporated the company's most significant technical innovation, an electronically operated exhaust valve. This varied the height of the port according to rpm, to give flexibility lower in the range while maintaining peak output at high revs. But on the OW48, the original cylindrical exhaust valve was replaced by a more efficient gullotine type.

The other major change was to the chassis, which for the first time on a Yamaha GP machine was made from lightweight aluminium tubing, of square section. Cast alloy wheels with a trio of disc brakes had been used on YZR500s for several seasons.

Midway through the 1980 season Yamaha wheeled out its updated OW48R, the R indicating reversed cylinders. Each of the outer two cylinders was switched around so that its intake port and carburettor faced forward. The outer exhaust pipes were now straight, which, as MZ had discovered in the late 1950s, improved torque. But even with this refinement, the peaky Yamaha engine needed to be turning at 10,000rpm to accelerate hard out of corners, while Suzuki's disc valve RG500 would pull from half that rpm. Top speed was no better than the RG500's, or Kawasaki's KR500, but Roberts' riding and setting-up skills went a long way in ensuring the OW48s' success.

For 1981, Roberts moved on to the OW54, featuring a V-four engine layout and disc valve induction. The OW48R shown here was raced by Sheene early in 1981, then by Dutch rider Boet Van Dulmen and in the 1982 Senior TT by Charlie Williams, where he set a lap record of 115.08mph after stopping to straighten a kinked fuel pipe and finished 13th.

▲ The Kayaba front fork is equipped with an anti-dive system activated by braking pressure. Yamaha was a modern pioneer of monoshock rear suspension, fitting it to GP 500s from 1974.

▼ The outer two cylinders are reversed to create a straighter exhaust path. When photographed this engine had earlier cylindrical exhaust valves: the works gullotine type giving more power have since been re-fitted.

Engine type: In-line four-cylinder, piston port, two-stroke
Capacity: 498cc
Bore and stroke: 56mm x 50.6mm
Compression ratio: n/a
Fuel system: Four 38mm Mikuni carburettors
Power: 102PS @ 11,500rpm
Gearbox: Six-speed
Suspension: Front, telescopic fork. Rear, monoshock
Brakes: Discs front and rear
Dry weight: 130kg
Top speed: 190mph

LIGHTER METAL
To reduce weight, Yamaha adopted an aluminium frame for 1980, preferring to use square-section rather than round tubing. This chassis was superseded by the company's far stronger Deltabox aluminium frame in 1983.

KREIDLER

50cc · 1983

With seven world titles, Kreidler was the most successful marque in the 50cc class during its period in the GP programme from 1962 to 1983. Racing to promote its road-going 50cc two-stroke lightweights, the German factory provided stiff opposition to Suzuki in the early years, being series runner-up in 1962 and 1963.

As development and spending escalated, Kreidler faded from the GP scene and concentrated on speed records, reaching 131mph in 1965. But in 1971, after Japanese makers had lost interest in the 'tiddler' class, the marque bounced back to better Derbi and score the first of its world championships.

By that time the race team was being run from Amsterdam, under the banner of Kreidler's Dutch agent Van Veen, who marketed engine race-kits and production racers as well as fielding its successful GP team with Jan de Vries as its number one rider.

Owning much to the brilliance of German two-stroke specialist Jorg Möller, the 1971 engine continued Kreidler's tradition of using disc valve induction and a single forward-facing cylinder. But it now had liquid cooling and an output of 17.5PS compared with the 14PS achieved in the mid-1960s.

De Vries won a second crown in 1973 and Henk van Kessel took the 1974 championship, prompting Derbi's former champion Angel Nieto to join the Van Veen team and secure his fourth 50cc title in the next year. He then joined Bultaco, which had bought out the Italian Piovaticci 50cc team, and took three titles. But Kreidler remained in contention and collected three more titles, gained by Eugenio Lazzarini and Stefan Dorflinger.

Ongoing development of the tiny machines included the adoption of a trellis-type spine frame and boosting of the engine's output to a phenomenal 20PS. Much of the gain was due to advanced metallurgy and development of electronic ignition impervious to ultra-high rpm.

The Kreidler Van Veen shown here was raced in the final phase of 50cc GP racing, its engine being prepared by leading tuner Harold Bartol and installed in a Schimmel frame. The six-speed gearbox internals are by Austrian maker Schafleitner.

▲ By the time 50cc GP racing was phased out in favour of an 80cc class for 1984, the tiny two-stroke engines had been developed to produce the equivalent of 400bhp per litre.

▼ Tiny engine and frame emphasise comparatively large 18-inch cast wheels. Only a few 50cc racers felt the need for twin disc front brakes, as seen on this machine.

Engine type: Single-cylinder, liquid-cooled, disc-valve two-stroke
Capacity: 50cc
Bore and stroke: 40mm x 39.7mm
Compression ratio: 9.8:1
Fuel system: 28mm Mikuni carburettor
Power: 20PS @ 16,000rpm
Gearbox: Six-speed
Suspension: Front, telescopic fork. Rear, swingarm with twin shock absorbers
Brakes: Drums front and rear
Dry weight: 85kg
Top speed: 120mph

FINAL-PHASE FIFTY
Henk van Veen's Holland-based company took over racing Kreidlers after the works team's withdrawal in the 1960s. After the German factory closed in 1982, Kreidler-powered machines raced on in 50 and 80cc events.

NORTON JPS

588cc · 1991

Few people could have foreseen Norton's amazing run of road racing successes from 1988 to 1993. The unexpected come-back of a once-legendary British factory was due to its piston-less rotary engine, under development for road use since the 1970s.

Norton engineer Brian Crighton initiated the racing project in 1987. In early tests, the free-revving air-cooled Wankel engine produced over 130PS. It won its first race in 1987 and televised 1988 UK Formula One series successes attracted major backing from the John Player Special tobacco brand in whose colours new liquid-cooled Nortons were raced from 1989.

Team riders Trevor Nation and Steve Spray screamed their black RCW 588s to victory in two major 1989 UK championships, and interest in Norton greatly boosted spectator numbers. Isle of Man TT results were disappointing in 1989 but in the 1990 Senior race, Nation was runner up to Carl Fogarty's Honda.

Seasoned rider Ron Haslam replaced Spray for 1991 and helped develop the new NRS588 with chassis expert Ron Williams. Its finest hour came with a record-breaking win in the 1992 Senior TT by Steve Hislop on a machine not in John Player colours. With new sponsor Duckhams Oils, a reformed rotary team enjoyed British short circuit success in 1994 but rotary engines were then outlawed by the UK governing body.

Neither four-stroke or two-stroke, Norton's valve-less rotary engine based on NSU Wankel patents was difficult to classify in terms of cubic capacity for racing. At first the FIM rated it at 1000cc, but Britain's ACU accepted Norton's 588cc rating based on the combined capacity of two combustion chambers, one for each three-chamber rotor. As a result, the rotary could race against 750cc four-strokes in UK TT Superbike events.

In 1991, with changes to the GP formulae being mooted, the FIM allowed the crowd-pulling Norton to contest the 500cc British GP and Ron Haslam finished 12th among four cylinder two-strokes. The compact power unit contains two side-by-side rotors with primary drive to the six speed gearbox by belt. Strong on acceleration, the rotary also offers a wide power band.

▲ Twin spar aluminium frame with monoshock rear suspension is by Harris Performance Products. Seat support is made from ultra-light carbon fibre reinforced moulding.

▼ A secondary tube feeding into the rear portion of the exhaust system from below is used to draw cool air through the rotary engine, which runs at extremely high temperatures.

Engine type: Twin-rotor, liquid-cooled, Wankel rotary
Capacity: 588cc
Compression ratio: 9:1
Fuel system: Two 35mm Keihin carburettors
Power: 135PS @ 9,800rpm
Gearbox: Six-speed
Suspension: Front, telescopic fork. Rear, monoshock
Brakes: Discs front and rear
Dry weight: 140kg
Top speed: 190mph

GRAND PRIX GUEST STAR
Not strictly a GP-class racer, the Norton rotary was permitted to run against 500cc two-srokes at the 1991 British GP. This example was raced by Robert Dunlop in TT and Irish events.